First Published In 2021 By Riley Parry
© Riley Parry
The information provided herein is stated to be truthful and consistent, of inattention or otherwise, by any usage or abuse of any policies, proc within is the solitary and utter responsibility of the recipient reader. Under no circumstances will any legal responsibility or blame be held against the publisher for any reparation, damages, or monetary loss due to the information herein, either directly or indirectly. Respective authors own all copyrights not held by the publisher.

The information herein is offered for informational purposes solely and is universal as so. The presentation of the information is without contract or any type of guarantee assurance. The trademarks that are used are without any consent, and the publication of the trademark is without permission or backing by the trademark owner. All trademarks and brands within this book are for clarifying purposes only and are the owned by the owners themselves, not affiliated with this document.

CONTENTS

INTRODUCTION 6
- The Benefits of an Air Frying Oven 6
- What Foods Can You Cook in an Air Frying Oven? 6
- Three Tips for the Best Air Fryer Oven Cooking Results 6

VEGETABLES AND VEGETARIAN 8
- Air-fried Potato Salad 8
- Lentil "meat" Loaf 9
- Empty-the-refrigerator Roasted Vegetables 10
- Salt And Pepper Baked Potatoes 11
- Parmesan Asparagus 12
- Baked Mac And Cheese 13
- Roasted Eggplant Halves With Herbed Ricotta 14
- Roasted Corn Salad 15
- Asparagus Fries 16
- Florentine Stuffed Tomatoes 17
- Spicy Sweet Potatoes 18
- Salmon Salad With Steamboat Dressing 19

SNACKS APPETIZERS AND SIDES 20
- Fried Mozzarella Sticks 20
- Cheesy Zucchini Squash Casserole 21
- Fiery Bacon-wrapped Dates 22
- Brazilian Cheese Bread (pão De Queijo) 23
- Grilled Ham & Muenster Cheese On Raisin Bread 24
- Fried Green Tomatoes 25
- Sweet Potato Fries With Sweet And Spicy Dipping Sauce 26
- Cinnamon Pita Chips 27
- Arancini 28

Okra Chips 29
Sausage Cheese Pinwheels 30
Granola Three Ways 31

POULTRY 33
Chicken Pot Pie 33
Turkey Sausage Cassoulet 34
Crispy "fried" Chicken 35
Chicken Adobo 36
Italian Baked Chicken 37
Chicken Cordon Bleu 38
Golden Seasoned Chicken Wings 39
Chicken Potpie 40
I Forgot To Thaw—garlic Capered Chicken Thighs 41
Oven-crisped Chicken 42
Sweet-and-sour Chicken 43
Chicken Ranch Roll-ups 45

LUNCH AND DINNER 46
Slow Cooker Chicken Philly Cheesesteak Sandwich 46
Couscous-stuffed Poblano Peppers 47
Kasha Loaf 49
Spanako Pizza 50
Easy Oven Lasagne 51
Baked Tomato Casserole 52
Yeast Dough For Two Pizzas 53
Broiled Chipotle Tilapia With Avocado Sauce 54
Honey-glazed Ginger Pork Meatballs 55
Connecticut Garden Chowder 56
Lima Bean And Artichoke Casserole 57
Sun-dried Tomato Pizza 58

FISH AND SEAFOOD ... 59
- Spicy Fish Street Tacos With Sriracha Slaw ... 59
- Blackened Catfish ... 61
- Light Trout Amandine ... 62
- Oysters Broiled In Wine Sauce ... 63
- Pecan-crusted Tilapia ... 64
- Sesame-crusted Tuna Steaks ... 65
- Quick Shrimp Scampi ... 66
- Almond Crab Cakes ... 67
- Crispy Pecan Fish ... 68
- Coconut Shrimp ... 69
- Lemon-dill Salmon Burgers ... 70
- Lemon-roasted Salmon Fillets ... 71

DESSERTS ... 72
- Frozen Brazo De Mercedes ... 72
- Orange-glazed Brownies ... 73
- Scones ... 74
- Easy Churros ... 75
- Bourbon Bread Pudding ... 76
- Blueberry Crumbles ... 77
- Chocolate Cupcakes With Salted Caramel Buttercream ... 78
- Baked Custard ... 80
- Not Key Lime, Lime Pie ... 81
- Easy Peach Turnovers ... 82
- Chewy Coconut Cake ... 83
- Blackberry Pie ... 84

BREAKFAST ... 85
- Green Onion Pancakes ... 85
- Yogurt Bread ... 86

Lemon Blueberry Scones 87
Chocolate Chip Banana Muffins 88
Cinnamon Toast 89
Popovers 90
Coffee Cake 91
Spinach, Tomato & Feta Quiche 92
Flaky Granola 94
Strawberry Pie 95
Yogurt Cheese Spread 96
Walnut Pancake 97

BEEF PORK AND LAMB 98
Crispy Lamb Shoulder Chops 98
California Burritos 99
Slow Cooked Carnitas 100
Beef Vegetable Stew 101
Smokehouse-style Beef Ribs 102
Chicken Fried Steak 103
Lamb Curry 104
Beer-baked Pork Tenderloin 105
Crispy Smoked Pork Chops 106
Bourbon Broiled Steak 107
Stuffed Bell Peppers 108
Traditional Pot Roast 109

RECIPES INDEX 110

INTRODUCTION

An air fryer oven is a full-sized oven that features an air fry cooking mode integrated within the oven cavity. With this innovative technology, you can now enjoy all of the benefits of air fry no matter what kind of range you're looking for - induction, gas, or electric. By using a high-powered fan to circulate hot air around the food at a high speed, our in-range air fry feature cooks ingredients to a perfectly crisped finish.

The Benefits of an Air Frying Oven

An air frying oven uses little to no oil to create a flavorful and crunchy texture on foods and boasts all of the same benefits as a standalone air fryer - with some additional conveniences.

1. The air fry feature is integrated right into your oven, eliminating the need to store an extra appliance or take up valuable counter space.
2. An air frying oven has more capacity, saving you time and allowing you to cook more food at once so that there's always enough for the whole family.
3. A Frigidaire Air Fry Oven does more than just air fry, so one appliance works harder for you. Enjoy other features such as Even Baking with True Convection, Fast Steam Cleaning, and Smudge-Proof® Stainless Steel.

What Foods Can You Cook in an Air Frying Oven?

An air fryer oven does a delicious job at cooking most traditional deep-fried foods and these are some of our favorites:

- Sweet Potato or French fries
- Chicken wings or tenders
- Zucchini fries
- Onion rings
- Pepperoni pizza rolls
- Mac 'n' cheese
- Brussel sprouts

Three Tips for the Best Air Fryer Oven Cooking Results

Just like any form of cooking, air frying can be an art form. Use these helpful tips to make sure your meal turns out perfectly browned and crisp every time.

1. Don't overload the pan or tray. If ingredients are packed too close together, the hot air won't be able to reach all the edges and create that perfect fried crispiness.
2. Double-check your recipe. The proper cooking time and the temperature are essential for the best air fryer oven results. Also, make sure you are using the correct amount of oil. With no oil, food will not be as crisp, and the texture can turn gritty, but too much oil and food can turn out soggy. Be sure to use cooking oils or sprays that can stand up to high temperatures like avocado, grapeseed, and peanut oils.
3. Use the correct tray. The optional ReadyCook™ Air Fry Tray lets air circulate around each piece of food, creating quicker, crispier results. When using the Air Fry Tray, put a baking sheet on a rack or two below it. This keeps drips and crumbs from landing on the oven bottom, where they can burn and create smoke. For additional protection, place some foil-lined parchment paper on the baking sheet.

VEGETABLES AND VEGETARIAN

Air-fried Potato Salad

Servings: 4
Cooking Time: 15 Minutes

Ingredients:
- 1⅓ pounds Yellow potatoes, such as Yukon Golds, cut into ½-inch chunks
- 1 large Sweet white onion(s), such as Vidalia, chopped into ½-inch pieces
- 1 tablespoon plus 2 teaspoons Olive oil
- ¾ cup Thinly sliced celery
- 6 tablespoons Regular or low-fat mayonnaise (gluten-free, if a concern)
- 2½ tablespoons Apple cider vinegar
- 1½ teaspoons Dijon mustard (gluten-free, if a concern)
- ¾ teaspoon Table salt
- ¼ teaspoon Ground black pepper

Directions:
1. Preheat the toaster oven to 400°F.
2. Toss the potatoes, onion(s), and oil in a large bowl until the vegetables are glistening with oil.
3. When the machine is at temperature, transfer the vegetables to the air fryer oven, spreading them out into as even a layer as you can. Air-fry for 15 minutes, tossing and rearranging the vegetables every 3 minutes so that all surfaces get exposed to the air currents, until the vegetables are tender and even browned at the edges.
4. Pour the contents of the air fryer oven into a serving bowl. Cool for at least 5 minutes or up to 30 minutes. Add the celery, mayonnaise, vinegar, mustard, salt, and pepper. Stir well to coat. The potato salad can be made in advance; cover and refrigerate for up to 4 days.

Lentil "meat" Loaf

Servings: 4
Cooking Time: 55 Minutes

Ingredients:
- Oil spray (hand-pumped)
- 2 (14-ounce) cans low-sodium lentils, drained and rinsed
- ½ sweet onion, chopped
- 1 carrot, shredded
- 1 teaspoon minced garlic
- 1½ cups seasoned bread crumbs
- ½ cup vegetable broth
- 3 tablespoons tomato paste
- ¼ teaspoon sea salt
- ⅛ teaspoon freshly ground black pepper
- 3 tablespoons ketchup
- 2 tablespoons maple syrup
- 1 tablespoon apple cider vinegar

Directions:
1. Place the rack in position 1 and preheat oven to 375°F on BAKE for 5 minutes.
2. Lightly coat a 9-by-5-inch loaf pan with oil spray.
3. Place the lentils, onion, carrot, and garlic in a food processor and pulse until very well mixed. Transfer the mixture to a large bowl and add the bread crumbs, vegetable broth, tomato paste, salt, and pepper. Mix well. If the mixture doesn't hold together, add vegetable broth by tablespoons until it does.
4. Press the lentil mixture into the loaf pan.
5. In a small bowl, stir the ketchup, maple syrup, and vinegar together. Spread the glaze over the lentil loaf.
6. Bake for 55 minutes until lightly browned. Serve.

Empty-the-refrigerator Roasted Vegetables

Servings: 4
Cooking Time: 35 Minutes

Ingredients:
- 3 cups assorted fresh vegetables, cut into 1 × 1-inch pieces
- 2 garlic cloves, minced
- 2 tablespoons olive oil
- 3 tablespoons dry white wine
- Salt and freshly ground black pepper to taste
- 1 tablespoon chopped fresh basil
- 1 tablespoon chopped fresh oregano
- 1 tablespoon chopped fresh parsley

Directions:
1. Preheat the toaster oven to 400° F.
2. Combine all the ingredients with 2 tablespoons water in a 1-quart 8½ × 8½ × 4-inch ovenproof baking dish, mixing well. Cover the dish with aluminum foil.
3. BAKE, covered, for 25 minutes, until the vegetables are tender. Remove from the oven and stir to blend the vegetables and sauce.
4. BROIL, uncovered, for 10 minutes, or until lightly browned.

Salt And Pepper Baked Potatoes

Servings: 40
Cooking Time: 4 Minutes

Ingredients:
- 1 to 2 tablespoons olive oil
- 4 medium russet potatoes (about 9 to 10 ounces each)
- salt and coarsely ground black pepper
- butter, sour cream, chopped fresh chives, scallions or bacon bits (optional)

Directions:
1. Preheat the toaster oven to 400°F.
2. Rub the olive oil all over the potatoes and season them generously with salt and coarsely ground black pepper. Pierce all sides of the potatoes several times with the tines of a fork.
3. Air-fry for 40 minutes, turning the potatoes over halfway through the cooking time.
4. Serve the potatoes, split open with butter, sour cream, fresh chives, scallions or bacon bits.

Parmesan Asparagus

Servings: 2
Cooking Time: 5 Minutes

Ingredients:
- 1 bunch asparagus, stems trimmed
- 1 teaspoon olive oil
- salt and freshly ground black pepper
- ¼ cup coarsely grated Parmesan cheese
- ½ lemon

Directions:
1. Preheat the toaster oven to 400°F.
2. Toss the asparagus with the oil and season with salt and freshly ground black pepper.
3. Transfer the asparagus to the air fryer oven and air-fry at 400°F for 5 minutes, turn the asparagus once or twice during the cooking process.
4. When the asparagus is cooked to your liking, sprinkle the asparagus generously with the Parmesan cheese and close the air fryer oven again. Let the asparagus sit for 1 minute in the turned-off air fryer oven. Then, remove the asparagus, transfer it to a serving dish and finish with a grind of black pepper and a squeeze of lemon juice.

Baked Mac And Cheese

Servings: 4
Cooking Time: 45 Minutes

Ingredients:
- Oil spray (hand-pumped)
- 1½ cups whole milk, room temperature
- ½ cup heavy (whipping) cream, room temperature
- 1 cup shredded cheddar cheese
- 4 ounces cream cheese, room temperature
- ½ teaspoon dry mustard
- ⅛ teaspoon sea salt
- ⅛ teaspoon freshly ground black pepper
- 1¼ cups dried elbow macaroni
- ¼ cup bread crumbs
- 2 tablespoons grated Parmesan cheese
- 1 tablespoon salted butter, melted

Directions:
1. Place the rack in position 1 and preheat the toaster oven to 375°F on CONVECTION BAKE for 5 minutes.
2. Lightly coat an 8-inch-square baking dish with the oil spray.
3. In a large bowl, stir the milk, cream, cheddar, cream cheese, mustard, salt, and pepper until well combined.
4. Transfer the mixture to the baking dish, stir in the macaroni and cover tightly with foil.
5. Bake for 35 minutes.
6. While the macaroni is baking, in a small bowl, stir the bread crumbs, Parmesan, and butter to form coarse crumbs. Set aside.
7. Take the baking dish out of the oven, uncover, stir, and evenly cover with the bread crumb mixture.
8. Bake uncovered for an additional 10 minutes until the pasta is tender, bubbly, and golden brown. Serve.

Roasted Eggplant Halves With Herbed Ricotta

Servings: 3
Cooking Time: 20 Minutes

Ingredients:
- 3 5- to 6-ounce small eggplants, stemmed
- Olive oil spray
- ¼ teaspoon Table salt
- ¼ teaspoon Ground black pepper
- ½ cup Regular or low-fat ricotta
- 1½ tablespoons Minced fresh basil leaves
- 1¼ teaspoons Minced fresh oregano leaves
- Honey

Directions:
1. Preheat the toaster oven to 325°F (or 330°F, if that's the closest setting).
2. Cut the eggplants in half lengthwise. Set them cut side up on your work surface. Using the tip of a paring knife, make a series of slits about three-quarters down into the flesh of each eggplant half; work at a 45-degree angle to the (former) stem across the vegetable and make the slits about ½ inch apart. Make a second set of equidistant slits at a 90-degree angle to the first slits, thus creating a crosshatch pattern in the vegetable.
3. Generously coat the cut sides of the eggplants with olive oil spray. Sprinkle the salt and pepper over the cut surfaces.
4. Set the eggplant halves cut side up in the air fryer oven with as much air space between them as possible. Air-fry undisturbed for 20 minutes, or until soft and golden.
5. Use kitchen tongs to gently transfer the eggplant halves to serving plates or a platter. Cool for 5 minutes.
6. Whisk the ricotta, basil, and oregano in a small bowl until well combined. Top the eggplant halves with this mixture. Drizzle the halves with honey to taste before serving warm.

Roasted Corn Salad

Servings: 3
Cooking Time: 15 Minutes

Ingredients:
- 3 4-inch lengths husked and de-silked corn on the cob
- Olive oil spray
- 1 cup Packed baby arugula leaves
- 12 Cherry tomatoes, halved
- Up to 3 Medium scallion(s), trimmed and thinly sliced
- 2 tablespoons Lemon juice
- 1 tablespoon Olive oil
- 1½ teaspoons Honey
- ¼ teaspoon Mild paprika
- ¼ teaspoon Dried oregano
- ¼ teaspoon, plus more to taste Table salt
- ¼ teaspoon Ground black pepper

Directions:
1. Preheat the toaster oven to 400°F.
2. When the machine is at temperature, lightly coat the pieces of corn on the cob with olive oil spray. Set the pieces of corn in the air fryer oven with as much air space between them as possible. Air-fry undisturbed for 15 minutes, or until the corn is charred in a few spots.
3. Use kitchen tongs to transfer the corn to a wire rack. Cool for 15 minutes.
4. Cut the kernels off the ears by cutting the fat end off each piece so it will stand up straight on a cutting board, then running a knife down the corn. (Or you can save your fingers and buy a fancy tool to remove kernels from corn cobs. Check it out at online kitchenware stores.) Scoop the kernels into a serving bowl.
5. Chop the arugula into bite-size bits and add these to the kernels. Add the tomatoes and scallions, too. Whisk the lemon juice, olive oil, honey, paprika, oregano, salt, and pepper in a small bowl until the honey dissolves. Pour over the salad and toss well to coat, tasting for extra salt before serving.

Asparagus Fries

Servings: 4
Cooking Time: 5 Minutes

Ingredients:
- 12 ounces fresh asparagus spears with tough ends trimmed off
- 2 egg whites
- ¼ cup water
- ¾ cup panko breadcrumbs
- ¼ cup grated Parmesan cheese, plus 2 tablespoons
- ¼ teaspoon salt
- oil for misting or cooking spray

Directions:
1. Preheat the toaster oven to 390°F.
2. In a shallow dish, beat egg whites and water until slightly foamy.
3. In another shallow dish, combine panko, Parmesan, and salt.
4. Dip asparagus spears in egg, then roll in crumbs. Spray with oil or cooking spray.
5. Place a layer of asparagus in air fryer oven, leaving just a little space in between each spear. Stack another layer on top, crosswise. Air-fry at 390°F for 5 minutes, until crispy and golden brown.
6. Repeat to cook remaining asparagus.

Florentine Stuffed Tomatoes

Servings: 12
Cooking Time: 2 Minutes

Ingredients:
- 1 cup frozen spinach, thawed and squeezed dry
- ¼ cup toasted pine nuts
- ¼ cup grated mozzarella cheese
- ½ cup crumbled feta cheese
- ½ cup coarse fresh breadcrumbs
- 1 tablespoon olive oil
- salt and freshly ground black pepper
- 2 to 3 beefsteak tomatoes, halved horizontally and insides scooped out

Directions:
1. Combine the spinach, pine nuts, mozzarella and feta cheeses, breadcrumbs, olive oil, salt and freshly ground black pepper in a bowl. Spoon the mixture into the tomato halves. You should have enough filling for 2 to 3 tomatoes, depending on how big they are.
2. Preheat the toaster oven to 350°F.
3. Place three or four tomato halves (depending on whether you're using 2 or 3 tomatoes and how big they are) into the air fryer oven and air-fry for 12 minutes. The tomatoes should be soft but still manageable and the tops should be lightly browned. Repeat with second batch if necessary.
4. Let the tomatoes cool for just a minute or two before serving.

Spicy Sweet Potatoes

Servings: 4
Cooking Time: 25 Minutes

Ingredients:
- 2 sweet potatoes, peeled and sliced into 1-inch rounds
- 1 tablespoon vegetable oil
- Seasonings:
- ½ teaspoon each: grated nutmeg, ground cinnamon, cardamom, and ginger
- Salt and freshly ground black pepper to taste

Directions:
1. Preheat the toaster oven to 400° F.
2. Brush the potato slices with oil and set aside.
3. Combine the seasonings in a 1-quart 8½ × 8½ × 4-inch ovenproof baking dish and add the potato slices. Toss to coat well and adjust the seasonings to taste. Cover the dish with aluminum foil.
4. BAKE for 25 minutes, or until the potatoes are tender.

Salmon Salad With Steamboat Dressing

Servings: 4
Cooking Time: 18 Minutes

Ingredients:
- ¼ teaspoon salt
- 1½ teaspoons dried dill weed
- 1 tablespoon fresh lemon juice
- 8 ounces fresh or frozen salmon fillet (skin on)
- 8 cups shredded romaine, Boston, or other leaf lettuce
- 8 spears cooked asparagus, cut in 1-inch pieces
- 8 cherry tomatoes, halved or quartered

Directions:
1. Mix the salt and dill weed together. Rub the lemon juice over the salmon on both sides and sprinkle the dill and salt all over. Refrigerate for 15 to 20 minutes.
2. Make Steamboat Dressing and refrigerate while cooking salmon and preparing salad.
3. Cook salmon in air fryer oven at 330°F for 18 minutes. Cooking time will vary depending on thickness of fillets. When done, salmon should flake with fork but still be moist and tender.
4. Remove salmon from air fryer oven and cool slightly. At this point, the skin should slide off easily. Cut salmon into 4 pieces and discard skin.
5. Divide the lettuce among 4 plates. Scatter asparagus spears and tomato pieces evenly over the lettuce, allowing roughly 2 whole spears and 2 whole cherry tomatoes per plate.
6. Top each salad with one portion of the salmon and drizzle with a tablespoon of dressing. Serve with additional dressing to pass at the table.

SNACKS APPETIZERS AND SIDES

Fried Mozzarella Sticks

Servings: 7
Cooking Time: 5 Minutes

Ingredients:
- 7 1-ounce string cheese sticks, unwrapped
- ½ cup All-purpose flour or tapioca flour
- 2 Large egg(s), well beaten
- 2¼ cups Seasoned Italian-style dried bread crumbs (gluten-free, if a concern)
- Olive oil spray

Directions:
1. Unwrap the string cheese and place the pieces in the freezer for 20 minutes (but not longer, or they will be too frozen to soften in the time given in the air fryer oven).
2. Preheat the toaster oven to 400°F.
3. Set up and fill three shallow soup plates or small pie plates on your counter: one for the flour, one for the egg(s), and one for the bread crumbs.
4. Dip a piece of cold string cheese in the flour until well coated (keep the others in the freezer). Gently tap off any excess flour, then set the stick in the egg(s). Roll it around to coat, let any excess egg mixture slip back into the rest, and set the stick in the bread crumbs. Gently roll it around to coat it evenly, even the ends. Now dip it back in the egg(s), then again in the bread crumbs, rolling it to coat well and evenly. Set the stick aside on a cutting board and coat the remaining pieces of string cheese in the same way.
5. Lightly coat the sticks all over with olive oil spray. Place them in the air fryer oven in one layer and air-fry undisturbed for 5 minutes, or until golden brown and crisp.
6. Remove from the machine and cool for 5 minutes. Use a nonstick-safe spatula to transfer the mozzarella sticks to a serving platter. Serve hot.

Cheesy Zucchini Squash Casserole

Servings: 12-14
Cooking Time: 30 Minutes

Ingredients:
- 1 Tablespoon olive oil
- 1 medium sweet onion, halved and thinly sliced
- 1 garlic clove, minced
- 1 pound zucchini, thinly sliced
- 1 pound yellow squash, thinly sliced
- 1 large egg
- 1/2 cup sour cream
- 1 cup shredded Cheddar cheese
- 1 cup shredded Swiss cheese
- 1 teaspoon thyme
- 1 teaspoon salt
- 1/2 teaspoon black pepper
- 3/4 cup seasoned panko crumbs
- 1 Tablespoon butter, melted

Directions:
1. Preheat the toaster oven to 350°F.
2. Heat olive oil in large skillet over medium-high heat. Add onion and garlic; cook 2 minutes. Stir in zucchini and yellow squash, cooking an additional 4 minutes or until squash is tender.
3. Beat egg and sour cream in large bowl until well blended. Stir in squash mixture, cheeses, thyme, salt and pepper. Pour into 8x8-inch baking dish.
4. Stir crumbs and butter in small bowl. Sprinkle over squash mixture.
5. Bake 25 to 30 minutes or until crumbs are golden brown and mixture is heated through.

Fiery Bacon-wrapped Dates

Servings: 16
Cooking Time: 6 Minutes

Ingredients:
- 8 Thin-cut bacon strips, halved widthwise (gluten-free, if a concern)
- 16 Medium or large Medjool dates, pitted
- 3 tablespoons (about ¾ ounce) Shredded semi-firm mozzarella
- 32 Pickled jalapeño rings

Directions:
1. Preheat the toaster oven to 400°F.
2. Lay a bacon strip half on a clean, dry work surface. Split one date lengthwise without cutting through it, so that it opens like a pocket. Set it on one end of the bacon strip and open it a bit. Place 1 teaspoon of the shredded cheese and 2 pickled jalapeño rings in the date, then gently squeeze it together without fully closing it (just to hold the stuffing inside). Roll up the date in the bacon strip and set it bacon seam side down on a cutting board. Repeat this process with the remaining bacon strip halves, dates, cheese, and jalapeño rings.
3. Place the bacon-wrapped dates bacon seam side down in the air fryer oven. Air-fry undisturbed for 6 minutes, or until crisp and brown.
4. Use kitchen tongs to gently transfer the wrapped dates to a wire rack or serving platter. Cool for a few minutes before serving.

Brazilian Cheese Bread (pão De Queijo)

Servings: 8
Cooking Time: 18 Minutes

Ingredients:
- 1 large egg, room temperature
- ⅓ cup olive oil
- ⅔ cups whole milk 1½ cups tapioca flour
- ½ cup feta cheese
- ¼ cup Parmesan cheese
- 1 teaspoon kosher salt
- ¼ teaspoon garlic powder
- Cooking spray

Directions:
1. Blend the egg, olive oil, milk, tapioca flour, feta, Parmesan, salt, and garlic powder in a stand mixer until smooth.
2. Spray the mini muffin pan with cooking spray.
3. Pour the batter into the muffin cups so they are ¾ full.
4. .Preheat the toaster oven to 380°F.
5. Place the muffin pan on the wire rack, then insert rack at mid position in the preheated oven.
6. Select the Bake function, adjust time to 18 minutes, and press Start/Pause.
7. Remove when done, then carefully pop the bread from the mini muffin tin and serve.

Grilled Ham & Muenster Cheese On Raisin Bread

Servings: 1
Cooking Time: 10 Minutes

Ingredients:
- 2 slices raisin bread
- 2 tablespoons butter, softened
- 2 teaspoons honey mustard
- 3 slices thinly sliced honey ham (about 3 ounces)
- 4 slices Muenster cheese (about 3 ounces)
- 2 toothpicks

Directions:
1. Preheat the toaster oven to 370°F.
2. Spread the softened butter on one side of both slices of raisin bread and place the bread, buttered side down on the counter. Spread the honey mustard on the other side of each slice of bread. Layer 2 slices of cheese, the ham and the remaining 2 slices of cheese on one slice of bread and top with the other slice of bread. Remember to leave the buttered side of the bread on the outside.
3. Transfer the sandwich to the air fryer oven and secure the sandwich with toothpicks.
4. Air-fry at 370°F for 5 minutes. Flip the sandwich over, remove the toothpicks and air-fry for another 5 minutes. Cut the sandwich in half and enjoy!!

Fried Green Tomatoes

Servings: 4
Cooking Time: 15 Minutes

Ingredients:
- 2 eggs
- ¼ cup buttermilk
- ½ cup cornmeal
- ½ cup breadcrumbs
- ¼ teaspoon salt
- 1½ pounds firm green tomatoes, cut in ¼-inch slices
- oil for misting or cooking spray
- Horseradish Drizzle
- ¼ cup mayonnaise
- ¼ cup sour cream
- 2 teaspoons prepared horseradish
- ½ teaspoon Worcestershire sauce
- ½ teaspoon lemon juice
- ⅛ teaspoon black pepper

Directions:
1. Mix all ingredients for Horseradish Drizzle together and chill while you prepare the green tomatoes.
2. Preheat the toaster oven to 390°F.
3. Beat the eggs and buttermilk together in a shallow bowl.
4. Mix cornmeal, breadcrumbs, and salt together in a plate or shallow dish.
5. Dip 4 tomato slices in the egg mixture, then roll in the breadcrumb mixture.
6. Mist one side with oil and place in air fryer oven, oil-side down, in a single layer.
7. Mist the top with oil.
8. Air-fry for 15 minutes, turning once, until brown and crispy.
9. Repeat steps 5 through 8 to cook remaining tomatoes.
10. Drizzle horseradish sauce over tomatoes just before serving.

Sweet Potato Fries With Sweet And Spicy Dipping Sauce

Servings: 2
Cooking Time: 20 Minutes

Ingredients:
- 1 large sweet potato (about 1 pound)
- 1 teaspoon vegetable or canola oil
- salt
- Sweet & Spicy Dipping Sauce
- ¼ cup light mayonnaise
- 1 tablespoon spicy brown mustard
- 1 tablespoon sweet Thai chili sauce
- ½ teaspoon sriracha sauce

Directions:
1. Scrub the sweet potato well and then cut it into ¼-inch French fries. (A mandolin slicer can really help with this.)
2. Preheat the toaster oven to 200°F.
3. Toss the sweet potato sticks with the oil and transfer them to the air fryer oven. Air-fry at 200°F for 10 minutes. Toss the fries with salt, increase the air fryer oven temperature to 400°F and air-fry for another 10 minutes.
4. To make the dipping sauce, combine all the ingredients in a small bowl and stir until combined.
5. Serve the sweet potato fries warm with the dipping sauce on the side.

Cinnamon Pita Chips

Servings: 4
Cooking Time: 6 Minutes

Ingredients:
- 2 tablespoons sugar
- 2 teaspoons cinnamon
- 2 whole 6-inch pitas, whole grain or white
- oil for misting or cooking spray

Directions:
1. Mix sugar and cinnamon together.
2. Cut each pita in half and each half into 4 wedges. Break apart each wedge at the fold.
3. Mist one side of pita wedges with oil or cooking spray. Sprinkle them all with half of the cinnamon sugar.
4. Turn the wedges over, mist the other side with oil or cooking spray, and sprinkle with the remaining cinnamon sugar.
5. Place pita wedges in air fryer oven and air-fry at 330°F for 2 minutes.
6. Cook 2 more minutes. If needed cook 2 more minutes, until crisp. Watch carefully because at this point they will cook very quickly.

Cheese Arancini

Servings: 8
Cooking Time: 12 Minutes

Ingredients:
- 1 cup Water
- ½ cup Raw white Arborio rice
- 1½ teaspoons Butter
- ¼ teaspoon Table salt
- 8 ¾-inch semi-firm mozzarella cubes (not fresh mozzarella)
- 2 Large egg(s), well beaten
- 1 cup Seasoned Italian-style dried bread crumbs (gluten-free, if a concern)
- Olive oil spray

Directions:
1. Combine the water, rice, butter, and salt in a small saucepan. Bring to a boil over medium-high heat, stirring occasionally. Cover, reduce the heat to very low, and simmer very slowly for 20 minutes.
2. Take the saucepan off the heat and let it stand, covered, for 10 minutes. Uncover it and fluff the rice. Cool for 20 minutes. (The rice can be made up to 1 hour in advance; keep it covered in its saucepan.)
3. Preheat the toaster oven to 375°F.
4. Set up and fill two shallow soup plates or small bowls on your counter: one with the beaten egg(s) and one with the bread crumbs.
5. With clean but wet hands, scoop up about 2 tablespoons of the cooked rice and form it into a ball. Push a cube of mozzarella into the middle of the ball and seal the cheese inside. Dip the ball in the egg(s) to coat completely, letting any excess egg slip back into the rest. Roll the ball in the bread crumbs to coat evenly but lightly. Set aside and continue making more rice balls.
6. Generously spray the balls with olive oil spray, then set them in the air fryer oven in one layer. They must not touch. Air-fry undisturbed for 10 minutes, or until crunchy and golden brown. If the machine is at 360°F, you may need to add 2 minutes to the cooking time.
7. Use a nonstick-safe spatula, and maybe a flatware spoon for balance, to gently transfer the balls to a wire rack. Cool for at least 5 minutes or up to 20 minutes before serving.

Okra Chips

Servings: 4
Cooking Time: 16 Minutes

Ingredients:
- 1¼ pounds Thin fresh okra pods, cut into 1-inch pieces
- 1½ tablespoons Vegetable or canola oil
- ¾ teaspoon Coarse sea salt or kosher salt

Directions:
1. Preheat the toaster oven to 400°F.
2. Toss the okra, oil, and salt in a large bowl until the pieces are well and evenly coated.
3. When the machine is at temperature, pour the contents of the bowl into the air fryer oven. Air-fry, tossing several times, for 16 minutes, or until crisp and quite brown (maybe even a little blackened on the thin bits).
4. Pour the contents of the air fryer oven onto a wire rack. Cool for a couple of minutes before serving.

Sausage Cheese Pinwheels

Servings: 16
Cooking Time: 22 Minutes

Ingredients:
- 1 sheet frozen puff pastry, about 9 inches square, thawed (½ of a 17.3-ounce package)
- ½ pound bulk sausage
- ¾ cup shredded cheddar cheese

Directions:
1. Preheat the toaster oven to 400°F. Grease a 12 x 12-inch baking pan.
2. Unfold the puff pastry on a lightly floured surface and roll into a 10 x 12-inch rectangle. Carefully spread the sausage over the surface of the rectangle to within ½ inch of all four edges. Sprinkle the cheese evenly over the sausage. Starting with the long side, roll up tightly and press the edges to seal.
3. Using a serrated knife, slice the roll into ½-inch-thick pieces. You will get about 16 slices. Place the slices, cut side up, in the prepared baking pan. Bake for 18 to 22 minutes or until golden and the sausage is cooked through.
4. Serve warm or at room temperature.

Granola Three Ways

Servings: 4
Cooking Time: 10 Minutes

Ingredients:
- Nantucket Granola
- ¼ cup maple syrup
- ¼ cup dark brown sugar
- 1 tablespoon butter
- 1 teaspoon vanilla extract
- 1 cup rolled oats
- ½ cup dried cranberries
- ½ cup walnuts, chopped
- ¼ cup pumpkin seeds
- ¼ cup shredded coconut
- Blueberry Delight
- ¼ cup honey
- ¼ cup light brown sugar
- 1 tablespoon butter
- 1 teaspoon lemon extract
- 1 cup rolled oats
- ½ cup sliced almonds
- ½ cup dried blueberries
- ¼ cup pumpkin seeds
- ¼ cup sunflower seeds
- Cherry Black Forest Mix
- ¼ cup honey
- ¼ cup light brown sugar
- 1 tablespoon butter
- 1 teaspoon almond extract
- 1 cup rolled oats
- ½ cup sliced almonds
- ½ cup dried cherries
- ¼ cup shredded coconut
- ¼ cup dark chocolate chips
- oil for misting or cooking spray

Directions:

1. Combine the syrup or honey, brown sugar, and butter in a small saucepan or microwave-safe bowl. Heat and stir just until butter melts and sugar dissolves. Stir in the extract.
2. Place all other dry ingredients in a large bowl. (For the Cherry Black Forest Mix, don't add the chocolate chips yet.)
3. Pour melted butter mixture over dry ingredients and stir until oat mixture is well coated.
4. Lightly spray a baking pan with oil or cooking spray.
5. Pour granola into pan and air-fry at 390°F for 5 minutes. Stir. Continue cooking for 5 minutes, stirring every minute or two, until golden brown. Watch closely. Once the mixture begins to brown, it will cook quickly.
6. Remove granola from pan and spread on wax paper. It will become crispier as it cools.
7. For the Cherry Black Forest Mix, stir in chocolate chips after granola has cooled completely.
8. Store in an airtight container.

POULTRY

Chicken Pot Pie

Servings: 4
Cooking Time: 65 Minutes

Ingredients:
- ¼ cup salted butter
- 1 small sweet onion, chopped
- 1 carrot, chopped
- 1 teaspoon minced garlic
- ¼ cup all-purpose flour
- 1 cup low-sodium chicken broth
- ¼ cup heavy (whipping) cream
- 2 cups diced store-bought rotisserie chicken
- 1 cup frozen peas
- Sea salt, for seasoning
- Freshly ground black pepper, for seasoning
- 1 unbaked store-bought pie crust

Directions:
1. Place the rack in position 1 and preheat the toaster oven to 350°F on BAKE for 5 minutes.
2. Melt the butter in a large saucepan over medium-high heat. Sauté the onion, carrot, and garlic until softened, about 12 minutes. Whisk in the flour to form a thick paste and whisk for 1 minute to cook.
3. Add the broth and whisk until thickened, about 2 minutes. Add the heavy cream, whisking to combine. Add the chicken and peas, and season with salt and pepper.
4. Transfer the filling to a 1½-quart casserole dish and top with the pie crust, tucking the edges into the sides of the casserole dish to completely enclose the filling. Cut 4 or 5 slits in the top of the crust.
5. Bake for 50 minutes until the crust is golden brown and the filling is bubbly. Serve.

Turkey Sausage Cassoulet

Servings: 4
Cooking Time: 52 Minutes

Ingredients:
- 3 turkey sausages
- 1 teaspoon olive oil
- ½ sweet onion
- 2 celery stalks, chopped
- 1 teaspoon minced garlic
- 2 (15-ounce) cans great northern beans, drained and rinsed
- 1 (15-ounce) can fire-roasted tomatoes
- 1 small sweet potato, diced
- 1 teaspoon dried thyme
- 2 cups kale, chopped
- Sea salt, for seasoning
- Freshly ground black pepper, for seasoning

Directions:
1. Preheat the toaster oven to 375°F on AIR FRY for 5 minutes.
2. Place the air-fryer basket in the baking tray and place the sausages in the basket. Prick them all over with a fork.
3. In position 2, air fry for 12 minutes until cooked through. Set the sausages aside to cool until you can handle them. Then cut into ¼-inch slices.
4. Change the oven to BAKE at 375°F and place the rack in position 1.
5. Heat the oil in a small skillet over medium-high heat and sauté the onion, celery, and garlic until softened.
6. Transfer the cooked vegetables to a 1½-quart casserole dish and stir in the sausage, beans, tomatoes, sweet potato, and thyme. Cover with foil or a lid.
7. Bake for 35 to 40 minutes until tender and any liquid is absorbed. Take the casserole out and stir in the kale. Let it sit for 10 minutes to wilt.
8. Season with salt and pepper, and serve.

Crispy "fried" Chicken

Servings: 4
Cooking Time: 14 Minutes

Ingredients:
- ¾ cup all-purpose flour
- ½ teaspoon paprika
- ¼ teaspoon black pepper
- ¼ teaspoon salt
- 2 large eggs
- 1½ cups panko breadcrumbs
- 1 pound boneless, skinless chicken tenders

Directions:
1. Preheat the toaster oven to 400°F.
2. In a shallow bowl, mix the flour with the paprika, pepper, and salt.
3. In a separate bowl, whisk the eggs; set aside.
4. In a third bowl, place the breadcrumbs.
5. Liberally spray the air fryer oven with olive oil spray.
6. Pat the chicken tenders dry with a paper towel. Dredge the tenders one at a time in the flour, then dip them in the egg, and toss them in the breadcrumb coating. Repeat until all tenders are coated.
7. Set each tender in the air fryer oven, leaving room on each side of the tender to allow for flipping.
8. When the air fryer oven is full, cook 4 to 7 minutes, flip, and cook another 4 to 7 minutes.
9. Remove the tenders and let cool 5 minutes before serving. Repeat until all tenders are cooked.

Chicken Adobo

Servings: 6
Cooking Time: 12 Minutes

Ingredients:
- 6 boneless chicken thighs
- ¼ cup soy sauce or tamari
- ½ cup rice wine vinegar
- 4 cloves garlic, minced
- ⅛ teaspoon crushed red pepper flakes
- ½ teaspoon black pepper

Directions:
1. Place the chicken thighs into a resealable plastic bag with the soy sauce or tamari, the rice wine vinegar, the garlic, and the crushed red pepper flakes. Seal the bag and let the chicken marinate at least 1 hour in the refrigerator.
2. Preheat the toaster oven to 400°F.
3. Drain the chicken and pat dry with a paper towel. Season the chicken with black pepper and liberally spray with cooking spray.
4. Place the chicken in the air fryer oven and air-fry for 9 minutes, turn over at 9 minutes and check for an internal temperature of 165°F, and cook another 3 minutes.

Italian Baked Chicken

Servings: 4
Cooking Time: 28 Minutes

Ingredients:
- 1 pound boneless, skinless chicken breasts
- ½ cup dry white wine
- 3 tablespoons olive oil
- 2 tablespoons white wine vinegar
- 2 tablespoons fresh lemon juice
- 2 teaspoons Italian seasoning
- 3 cloves garlic, minced
- ½ teaspoon kosher salt
- ¼ teaspoon freshly ground black pepper
- 4 slices salami, cut in half
- 3 tablespoons shredded Parmesan cheese

Directions:
1. If the chicken breasts are large and thick, slice each breast in half lengthwise. Place the chicken in a shallow baking dish.
2. Combine the white wine, olive oil, vinegar, lemon juice, Italian seasoning, garlic, salt, and pepper in a small bowl. Pour over the chicken breasts. Cover and refrigerate for 2 to 8 hours, turning the chicken occasionally to coat.
3. Preheat the toaster oven to 375 ºF.
4. Drain the chicken, discarding the marinade, and place the chicken in an ungreased 12 x 12-inch baking pan. Bake, uncovered, for 20 to 25 minutes or until the chicken is done and a meat thermometer registers 165 ºF. Place one slice salami (two pieces) on top of each piece of the chicken. Sprinkle the Parmesan evenly over the chicken breasts and broil for 2 to 3 minutes, or until the cheese is melted and starting to brown.

Chicken Cordon Bleu

Servings: 4
Cooking Time: 25 Minutes

Ingredients:
- Oil spray (hand-pumped)
- 4 (4-ounce) chicken breasts
- 4 teaspoons Dijon mustard
- 4 slices Gruyère cheese
- 4 slices lean ham
- 1 cup all-purpose flour
- 2 large eggs
- 1 cup bread crumbs
- ½ cup Parmesan cheese

Directions:
1. Preheat the toaster oven to 350°F on AIR FRY for 5 minutes.
2. Place the air-fryer basket in the baking tray and generously spray it with the oil.
3. Place a chicken breast flat on a clean work surface and cut along the length of the breast, almost in half, holding the knife parallel to the counter. Open the breast up like a book and place it between two pieces of plastic wrap. Pound the chicken breast to about ¼-inch thick with a rolling pin or mallet. Repeat with the remaining breasts.
4. Spread the mustard on each breast, place a piece of cheese and ham in the center, and fold the sides of the breast over the cheese and ham. Roll the breast up from the unfolded sides to form a sealed packet. Secure with a toothpick.
5. Repeat with the remaining breasts.
6. Sprinkle the flour on a plate and set it on your work surface.
7. In a small bowl, whisk the eggs until well beaten and place next to the flour.
8. In a medium bowl, stir the bread crumbs and Parmesan and place next to the eggs.
9. Dredge the chicken rolls in the flour, then egg, then the bread crumb mixture, making sure they are completely breaded.
10. Arrange the chicken in the basket and spray lightly all over with the oil.
11. In position 2, air fry for 25 minutes, turning halfway through, until golden brown. Serve.

Golden Seasoned Chicken Wings

Servings: 2
Cooking Time: 40 Minutes

Ingredients:
- Oil spray (hand-pumped)
- ¾ cup all-purpose flour
- 1 teaspoon garlic powder
- 1 teaspoon smoked paprika
- ½ teaspoon sea salt
- ¼ teaspoon freshly ground black pepper
- ¼ teaspoon onion powder
- 2 pounds chicken wing drumettes and flats

Directions:
1. Preheat the toaster oven to 400°F on AIR FRY for 5 minutes.
2. Place the air-fryer basket in the baking tray and spray it generously with the oil.
3. In a medium bowl, stir the flour, garlic powder, paprika, sea salt, pepper, and onion powder until well mixed.
4. Add half the chicken wings to the bowl and toss to coat with the flour.
5. Arrange the wings in the basket and spray both sides lightly with the oil.
6. In position 2, air fry for 20 minutes, turning halfway through, until golden brown and crispy.
7. Repeat with the remaining wings, covering the cooked wings loosely with foil to keep them warm. Serve.

Chicken Potpie

Servings: 4
Cooking Time: 48 Minutes

Ingredients:
- Pie filling:
- 1 tablespoon unbleached flour
- ½ cup evaporated skim milk
- 4 skinless, boneless chicken thighs, cut into 1-inch cubes
- 1 cup potatoes, peeled and cut into ½-inch pieces
- ½ cup frozen green peas
- ½ cup thinly sliced carrot
- 2 tablespoons chopped onion
- ½ cup chopped celery
- 1 teaspoon garlic powder
- Salt and freshly ground black pepper to taste
- 8 sheets phyllo pastry, thawed Olive oil

Directions:
1. Preheat the toaster oven to 400° F.
2. Whisk the flour into the milk until smooth in a 1-quart 8½ × 8½ × 4-inch ovenproof baking dish. Add the remaining filling ingredients and mix well. Adjust the seasonings to taste. Cover the dish with aluminum foil.
3. BAKE for 40 minutes, or until the carrot, potatoes, and celery are tender. Remove from the oven and uncover.
4. Place one sheet of phyllo pastry on top of the baked pie-filling mixture, bending the edges to fit the shape of the baking dish. Brush the sheet with olive oil. Add another sheet on top of it and brush with oil. Continue adding the remaining sheets, brushing each one, until the crust is completed. Brush the top with oil.
5. BAKE for 6 minutes, or until the phyllo pastry is browned.

I Forgot To Thaw—garlic Capered Chicken Thighs

Servings: 4
Cooking Time: 50 Minutes

Ingredients:
- 6 frozen skinless, boneless chicken thighs
- Garlic mixture:
- 3 garlic cloves, minced
- ¾ cup dry white wine
- 2 tablespoons capers
- ½ teaspoon paprika
- ¼ teaspoon ground cumin
- Salt and freshly ground black pepper to taste

Directions:
1. Preheat the toaster oven to 400° F.
2. Thaw the chicken as directed. Separate the pieces and add the garlic mixture, which has been combined in a small bowl, stirring well to coat. Cover the dish with aluminum foil.
3. BAKE for 30 minutes, or until the chicken is tender. Remove the cover and turn the chicken pieces, spooning the sauce over them.
4. BROIL for 8 minutes, or until the chicken is lightly browned.

Oven-crisped Chicken

Servings: 4
Cooking Time: 35 Minutes

Ingredients:
- Coating mixture:
- 1 cup cornmeal
- ¼ cup wheat germ
- 1 teaspoon paprika
- 1 teaspoon garlic powder
- Salt and butcher's pepper to taste
- 3 tablespoons olive oil
- 1 tablespoon spicy brown mustard
- 6 skinless, boneless chicken thighs

Directions:
1. Preheat the toaster oven to 375° F.
2. Combine the coating mixture ingredients in a small bowl and transfer to a plate, spreading the mixture evenly over the plate's surface. Set aside.
3. Whisk together the oil and mustard in a bowl. Add the chicken pieces and toss to coat thoroughly. Press both sides of each piece into the coating mixture to coat well. Chill in the refrigerator for 10 minutes. Transfer the chicken pieces to a broiling rack with a pan underneath.
4. BAKE, uncovered, for 35 minutes, or until the meat is tender and the coating is crisp and golden brown or browned to your preference.

Sweet-and-sour Chicken

Servings: 6
Cooking Time: 10 Minutes

Ingredients:
- 1 cup pineapple juice
- 1 cup plus 3 tablespoons cornstarch, divided
- ¼ cup sugar
- ¼ cup ketchup
- ¼ cup apple cider vinegar
- 2 tablespoons soy sauce or tamari
- 1 teaspoon garlic powder, divided
- ¼ cup flour
- 1 tablespoon sesame seeds
- ½ teaspoon salt
- ¼ teaspoon ground black pepper
- 2 large eggs
- 2 pounds chicken breasts, cut into 1-inch cubes
- 1 red bell pepper, cut into 1-inch pieces
- 1 carrot, sliced into ¼-inch-thick rounds

Directions:

1. In a medium saucepan, whisk together the pineapple juice, 3 tablespoons of the cornstarch, the sugar, the ketchup, the apple cider vinegar, the soy sauce or tamari, and ½ teaspoon of the garlic powder. Cook over medium-low heat, whisking occasionally as the sauce thickens, about 6 minutes. Stir and set aside while preparing the chicken.
2. Preheat the toaster oven to 370°F.
3. In a medium bowl, place the remaining 1 cup of cornstarch, the flour, the sesame seeds, the salt, the remaining ½ teaspoon of garlic powder, and the pepper.
4. In a second medium bowl, whisk the eggs.
5. Working in batches, place the cubed chicken in the cornstarch mixture to lightly coat; then dip it into the egg mixture, and return it to the cornstarch mixture. Shake off the excess and place the coated chicken in the air fryer oven. Spray with cooking spray and air-fry for 5 minutes, and spray with more cooking spray. Cook an additional 3 to 5 minutes, or until completely cooked and golden brown.
6. On the last batch of chicken, add the bell pepper and carrot to the air fryer oven and cook with the chicken.
7. Place the cooked chicken and vegetables into a serving bowl and toss with the sweet-and-sour sauce to serve.

Chicken Ranch Roll-ups

Servings: 4
Cooking Time: 10 Minutes

Ingredients:
- 4 6-inch flour tortillas
- Low-fat sour cream Chili powder
- Filling mixture:
- 1 cup cooked chopped chicken breast
- 4 tablespoons canned black beans
- 2 tablespoons shredded low-fat cheddar cheese
- 2 tablespoons finely chopped green bell pepper
- 2 tablespoons finely chopped onion
- 1 finely chopped plum tomato
- 2 tablespoons tomato salsa
- 1 seeded and chopped chili pepper
- Hot sauce or Salt and pepper

Directions:
1. Preheat the toaster oven to 350°F.
2. Blend filling ingredients together well in a bowl and season to taste.
3. Fill tortillas with equal portions of mixture, roll into cylinders and lay, seam side down, in an oiled or nonstick 8½" × 8½" × 2" square (cake) pan.
4. BAKE for 20 minutes or until browned and cheese is melted.

LUNCH AND DINNER

Slow Cooker Chicken Philly Cheesesteak Sandwich

Servings: 4
Cooking Time: 2 Minutes

Ingredients:
- 1 3/4 to 2 pounds chicken tenders
- 2 large green peppers, cut in strips
- 2 medium onions, sliced
- 1 1/2 tablespoons rotisserie seasoning
- 1/2 teaspoon salt
- 4 tablespoons Italian salad dressing
- 4 hoagie rolls, split
- 4 slices Cheddar or American cheese
- 1/4 cup banana pepper rings, optional
- Hot Sauce or ketchup, optional

Directions:
1. In slow cooker crock, combine chicken tenders, pepper strips and onion slices with rotisserie seasoning and salt.
2. Cook on HIGH for 2 to 2 1/2 hours or LOW for 4 to 5 hours.
3. Preheat the toaster oven broiler. Open rolls and place on a cookie sheet
4. Slice chicken tenders. Place back in slow cooker. With a slotted spoon, divide chicken, peppers and onions among rolls and drizzle with Italian dressing. Top with cheese slices.
5. Place under broiler until cheese is melted, about 2 minutes.
6. Serve with banana peppers, hot sauce or ketchup, if desired.

Couscous-stuffed Poblano Peppers

Servings: 6
Cooking Time: 35 Minutes

Ingredients:
- 2 tablespoons olive oil
- ⅔ cup Israeli couscous
- 1 ¼ cups vegetable broth or water
- Kosher salt and freshly ground black pepper
- ½ medium onion, chopped
- 2 cloves garlic, minced
- 1 teaspoon dried oregano leaves
- ½ teaspoon ground cumin
- 1 (14.5-ounce) can fire-roasted diced tomatoes, with liquid
- Nonstick cooking spray
- 3 large poblano peppers, halved lengthwise, seeds and stem removed
- 1 ½ cups shredded Mexican blend, pepper Jack, or sharp cheddar cheese
- Optional toppings: minced fresh cilantro, sliced jalapeño peppers, diced tomatoes, sliced green onions (white and green portions)

Directions:

1. Heat 1 tablespoon oil in a medium saucepan over medium heat. Add the couscous and cook, stirring frequently, until golden brown, 2 to 3 minutes. Stir in the broth and season with salt and pepper. Cover, reduce the heat to a simmer, and cook, stirring occasionally, for about 10 minutes or until the liquid is absorbed. Remove from the heat and let stand, covered, for 5 minutes. Remove the cover, stir, and set aside to cool.
2. Heat the remaining 1 tablespoon oil in a small saucepan over medium heat. Add the onion, and cook, stirring frequently, for 3 to 5 minutes or until tender. Stir in the garlic and cook for 30 seconds. Stir in the oregano and cumin and season with salt and pepper. Stir in the tomatoes and simmer for 5 minutes.
3. Preheat the toaster oven to 400°F. Spray a 9-inch square baking pan with nonstick cooking spray. Spoon about one-third of the tomato mixture into the prepared pan. Arrange the peppers, cut side up, in the pan.
4. Stir 1 cup of the cheese into the couscous. Spoon the couscous mixture into the peppers, mounding slightly. Spoon the remaining tomato mixture over the peppers. Cover the pan and bake for 30 minutes.
5. Uncover the pan and sprinkle with the remaining cheese. Bake for 5 minutes or until the cheese is melted.
6. Top as desired with any of the various topping choices.

Kasha Loaf

Servings: 4
Cooking Time: 30 Minutes

Ingredients:
- 1 cup whole grain kasha
- 2 cups tomato sauce or 3 2 8-ounce cans tomato sauce (add a small amount of water to make 4 2 cups)
- 3 tablespoons minced onion or scallions
- 1 tablespoon minced garlic
- 1 cup multigrain bread crumbs
- 1 egg
- 1 teaspoon paprika
- 1 teaspoon chili powder
- 1 teaspoon sesame oil

Directions:
1. Preheat the toaster oven to 400° F.
2. Combine all the ingredients in a bowl and transfer to an oiled or nonstick regular-size 4½ × 8½ × 2/4-inch loaf pan.
3. BAKE, uncovered, for 30 minutes, or until lightly browned.

Spanako Pizza

Servings: 2
Cooking Time: 30 Minutes

Ingredients:
- 8 sheets phyllo dough, thawed and folded in half
- 4 tablespoons olive oil
- 4 tablespoons grated Parmesan cheese
- Topping mixture:
- 1 10-ounce package frozen chopped spinach, thawed and well drained
- 1 plum tomato, finely chopped
- ¼ cup finely chopped onion
- ¼ cup shredded low-fat mozzarella cheese
- 3 tablespoons crumbled feta cheese or part-skim ricotta cheese
- 2 garlic cloves, minced
- Salt and freshly ground black pepper to taste

Directions:
1. Preheat the toaster oven to 375° F.
2. Layer the sheets of phyllo dough in an oiled or nonstick 9¾-inch-diameter baking pan, lightly brushing the top of each sheet with olive oil and folding in the corner edges to fit the pan.
3. Combine the topping mixture ingredients in a bowl and adjust the seasonings to taste. Spread the mixture on top of the phyllo pastry layers and sprinkle with the Parmesan cheese.
4. BAKE for 30 minutes, or until the cheese is melted and the topping is lightly browned. Remove carefully from the pan with a metal spatula.

Easy Oven Lasagne

Servings: 4
Cooking Time: 60 Minutes

Ingredients:
- 6 uncooked lasagna noodles, broken in half
- 1 15-ounce jar marinara sauce
- ½ pound ground turkey or chicken breast
- ½ cup part-skim ricotta cheese
- ½ cup shredded part-skim mozzarella cheese
- 2 tablespoons chopped fresh oregano leaves or 1 teaspoon dried oregano
- 2 tablespoons chopped fresh basil leaves or 1 teaspoon dried basil
- 1 tablespoon garlic cloves, minced
- ¼ cup grated Parmesan cheese
- Salt and freshly ground black pepper to taste

Directions:
1. Preheat the toaster oven to 375° F.
2. Layer in a 1-quart 8½ × 8½ × 4-inch ovenproof baking dish in this order: 6 lasagna noodle halves, ½ jar of the marinara sauce, ½ cup water, half of the ground meat, half of the ricotta and mozzarella cheeses, half of the oregano and basil leaves, and half of the minced garlic. Repeat the layer, starting with the noodles. Cover the dish with aluminum foil.
3. BAKE, covered, for 50 minutes, or until the noodles are tender. Uncover, sprinkle the top with Parmesan cheese and bake for another 10 minutes, or until the liquid is reduced and the top is browned.

Baked Tomato Casserole

Servings: 4
Cooking Time:45 Minutes

Ingredients:
- Casserole mixture:
- 1 medium onion, coarsely chopped
- 3 medium tomatoes, coarsely chopped
- 1 medium green pepper, coarsely chopped
- 2 garlic cloves, minced
- ½ teaspoon crushed oregano
- ½ teaspoon crushed basil
- 1 tablespoon extra virgin olive oil
- 2 tablespoons chopped fresh cilantro
- Salt and freshly ground black pepper
- 3 4 tablespoons grated Parmesan cheese
- ¼ cup multigrain bread crumbs

Directions:
1. Preheat the toaster oven to 400° F.
2. Combine the casserole mixture ingredients in a 1-quart 8½ × 8½ × 4-inch ovenproof baking dish. Adjust the seasonings to taste and cover with aluminum foil.
3. BAKE, covered, for 35 minutes, or until the tomatoes and pepper are tender. Remove from the oven, uncover, and sprinkle with the bread crumbs and Parmesan cheese.
4. BROIL for 10 minutes, or until the topping is lightly browned.

Yeast Dough For Two Pizzas

Servings: 8
Cooking Time: 20 Minutes

Ingredients:
- ¼ cup tepid water
- 1 cup tepid skim milk
- ½ teaspoon sugar
- 1 1¼-ounce envelope dry yeast
- 2 cups unbleached flour
- 1 tablespoon olive oil

Directions:
1. Preheat the toaster oven to 400° F.
2. Combine the water, milk, and sugar in a bowl. Add the yeast and set aside for 3 to 5 minutes, or until the yeast is dissolved.
3. Stir in the flour gradually, adding just enough to form a ball of the dough.
4. KNEAD on a floured surface until the dough is satiny, and then put the dough in a bowl in a warm place with a damp towel over the top. In 1 hour or when the dough has doubled in bulk, punch it down and divide it in half. Flatten the dough and spread it out to the desired thickness on an oiled or nonstick 9¾-inch-diameter pie pan. Spread with Homemade Pizza Sauce (recipe follows) and add any desired toppings.
5. BAKE for 20 minutes, or until the topping ingredients are cooked and the cheese is melted.

Broiled Chipotle Tilapia With Avocado Sauce

Servings: 2
Cooking Time: 10 Minutes

Ingredients:
- 1 small avocado, halved, pitted and peeled
- 3 tablespoons sour cream
- 1 teaspoon lime juice
- 2 1/2 teaspoons chipotle and roasted garlic seasoning, divided
- 1 tablespoon mayonnaise
- 1/2 pound tilapia fillets
- Chopped cilantro

Directions:
1. Using a chopper or small food processor, blend avocado, sour cream, lime juice and 1 1/2 teaspoons seasoning until smooth. Cover and refrigerate.
2. Spray toaster oven baking pan with nonstick cooking spray.
3. in small bowl, mix mayonnaise and remaining 1 teaspoon seasoning.
4. Brush mayonnaise mixture on both sides of tilapia fillets.
5. Place coated fish in pan.
6. Set toaster oven to BROIL. Broil fish for 10 minutes or until fish flakes with a fork.
7. Serve with avocado sauce and garnish with lime slices and cilantro, if desired.

Honey-glazed Ginger Pork Meatballs

Servings: 6
Cooking Time: 20 Minutes

Ingredients:
- 1 ½ pounds ground pork
- 2 tablespoons finely chopped onion
- 3 cloves garlic, minced
- 1 teaspoon minced fresh ginger
- 1 teaspoon sesame oil
- 1 large egg
- 3 tablespoons panko bread crumbs
- Kosher salt and freshly ground black pepper
- HONEY GINGER SAUCE
- 2 tablespoons sesame oil
- 1 tablespoon canola or vegetable oil
- 3 cloves garlic, minced
- 1 ½ tablespoons minced fresh ginger
- 3 tablespoons unseasoned rice wine vinegar
- 1 tablespoon reduced-sodium soy sauce
- 3 tablespoons honey
- 2 to 3 teaspoons garlic chili sauce
- 1 teaspoon cornstarch
- 1 tablespoon cold water
- 2 tablespoons minced fresh cilantro

Directions:
1. Preheat the toaster oven to 375°F. Line a 12 x 12-inch baking pan with nonstick aluminum foil (or if lining the pan with regular foil, spray it with nonstick cooking spray).
2. Combine the pork, onion, garlic, ginger, sesame oil, egg, and panko bread crumbs in a large bowl. Season with salt and pepper. Form into meatballs about 1 ½ inches in diameter. Place the meatballs in the prepared baking pan. Bake for 18 to 20 minutes or until done and a meat thermometer registers 160°F.
3. Make the Honey Ginger Sauce: Combine the sesame oil, canola oil, garlic, and ginger in a medium skillet over medium-high heat. Cook, stirring frequently, for 1 minute. Add the vinegar, soy sauce, honey, and chili sauce and bring to a boil. Whisk the cornstarch with the water in a small bowl. Stir the cornstarch mixture into the sauce and cook, stirring constantly, until thickened. Add the meatballs to the skillet and coat with the sauce. Sprinkle with the cilantro for serving.

Connecticut Garden Chowder

Servings: 4
Cooking Time: 60 Minutes

Ingredients:
- Soup:
- ½ cup peeled and shredded potato
- ½ cup shredded carrot
- ½ cup shredded celery 2 plum tomatoes, chopped
- 1 small zucchini, shredded
- 2 bay leaves
- ¼ teaspoon sage
- 1 teaspoon garlic powder
- Salt and butcher's pepper to taste
- Chowder base:
- 2 tablespoons reduced-fat cream cheese, at room temperature
- ½ cup fat-free half-and-half
- 2 tablespoons unbleached flour
- 2 tablespoons chopped fresh parsley

Directions:
1. Preheat the toaster oven to 375° F.
2. Combine the soup ingredients in a 1-quart 8½ × 8½ × 4-inch ovenproof baking dish, mixing well. Adjust the seasonings to taste.
3. BAKE, covered, for 40 minutes, or until the vegetables are tender.
4. Whisk the chowder mixture ingredients together until smooth. Add the mixture to the cooked soup ingredients and stir well to blend.
5. BAKE, uncovered for 20 minutes, or until the stock is thickened. Ladle the soup into individual soup bowls and garnish with the parsley.

Lima Bean And Artichoke Casserole

Servings: 4
Cooking Time: 40 Minutes

Ingredients:
- 1 15-ounce can lima beans, drained
- 1 6-ounce jar artichokes, marinated in olive oil (include the oil)
- ½ cup dry white wine
- 1 small onion, thinly sliced
- 2 medium carrots, thinly sliced
- 1 5-ounce can roasted peppers, drained and chopped
- ¼ teaspoon paprika
- ½ teaspoon ground cumin
- 1 teaspoon curry powder
- Salt and freshly ground black pepper to taste

Directions:
1. Preheat the toaster oven to 350° F.
2. Combine all the ingredients in a 1-quart 8½ × 8½ × 4-inch ovenproof baking dish, blending well. Adjust the seasonings to taste. Cover with aluminum foil.
3. BAKE, covered, for 40 minutes, or until the carrots and onion are tender.

Sun-dried Tomato Pizza

Servings: 4
Cooking Time: 25 Minutes

Ingredients:
- Tomato mixture:
- 1 cup chopped sun-dried tomatoes
- 2 tablespoons tomato paste
- 2 tablespoons olive oil
- 2 tablespoons chopped onion
- 2 garlic cloves, minced
- 1 teaspoon dried oregano
- 1 teaspoon dried basil
- Salt and red pepper flakes to taste
- 1 9-inch ready-made pizza crust
- 1 5-ounce can mushrooms
- ¼ cup pitted and sliced black olives
- ½ cup shredded low-fat mozzarella cheese

Directions:
1. Combine the tomato mixture ingredients with ½ cup water in an 8½ × 8½ × 2-inch square baking (cake) pan.
2. BROIL for 8 minutes, or until the tomatoes are softened. Remove from the oven and cool for 5 minutes.
3. Process the mixture in a blender or food processor until well blended. Spread on the pizza crust and layer with the mushrooms, olives, and cheese.
4. BAKE at 400° F. for 25 minutes, or until the cheese is melted.

FISH AND SEAFOOD

Spicy Fish Street Tacos With Sriracha Slaw

Servings: 2
Cooking Time: 5 Minutes

Ingredients:
- Sriracha Slaw:
- ½ cup mayonnaise
- 2 tablespoons rice vinegar
- 1 teaspoon sugar
- 2 tablespoons sriracha chili sauce
- 5 cups shredded green cabbage
- ¼ cup shredded carrots
- 2 scallions, chopped
- salt and freshly ground black pepper
- Tacos:
- ½ cup flour
- 1 teaspoon chili powder
- ½ teaspoon ground cumin
- 1 teaspoon salt
- freshly ground black pepper
- ½ teaspoon baking powder
- 1 egg, beaten
- ¼ cup milk
- 1 cup breadcrumbs
- 1 pound mahi-mahi or snapper fillets
- 1 tablespoon canola or vegetable oil
- 6 (6-inch) flour tortillas
- 1 lime, cut into wedges

Directions:

1. Start by making the sriracha slaw. Combine the mayonnaise, rice vinegar, sugar, and sriracha sauce in a large bowl. Mix well and add the green cabbage, carrots, and scallions. Toss until all the vegetables are coated with the dressing and season with salt and pepper. Refrigerate the slaw until you are ready to serve the tacos.
2. Combine the flour, chili powder, cumin, salt, pepper and baking powder in a bowl. Add the egg and milk and mix until the batter is smooth. Place the breadcrumbs in shallow dish.
3. Cut the fish fillets into 1-inch wide sticks, approximately 4-inches long. You should have about 12 fish sticks total. Dip the fish sticks into the batter, coating all sides. Let the excess batter drip off the fish and then roll them in the breadcrumbs, patting the crumbs onto all sides of the fish sticks. Set the coated fish on a plate or baking sheet until all the fish has been coated.
4. Preheat the toaster oven to 400°F.
5. Spray the coated fish sticks with oil on all sides. Spray or brush the inside of the air fryer oven with oil and transfer the fish to the air fryer oven. Place as many sticks as you can in one layer, leaving a little room around each stick. Place any remaining sticks on top, perpendicular to the first layer.
6. Air-fry the fish for 3 minutes. Turn the fish sticks over and air-fry for an additional 2 minutes.
7. While the fish is air-frying, warm the tortilla shells either in a 350°F oven wrapped in foil or in a skillet with a little oil over medium-high heat for a couple minutes. Fold the tortillas in half and keep them warm until the remaining tortillas and fish are ready.
8. To assemble the tacos, place two pieces of the fish in each tortilla shell and top with the sriracha slaw. Squeeze the lime wedge over top and dig in.

Blackened Catfish

Servings: 4
Cooking Time: 8 Minutes

Ingredients:
- 1 teaspoon paprika
- 1 teaspoon garlic powder
- 1 teaspoon onion powder
- 1 teaspoon ground dried thyme
- ½ teaspoon ground black pepper
- ⅛ teaspoon cayenne pepper
- ½ teaspoon dried oregano
- ⅛ teaspoon crushed red pepper flakes
- 1 pound catfish filets
- ½ teaspoon sea salt
- 2 tablespoons butter, melted
- 1 tablespoon extra-virgin olive oil
- 2 tablespoons chopped parsley
- 1 lemon, cut into wedges

Directions:
1. In a small bowl, stir together the paprika, garlic powder, onion powder, thyme, black pepper, cayenne pepper, oregano, and crushed red pepper flakes.
2. Pat the fish dry with paper towels. Season the filets with sea salt and then coat with the blackening seasoning.
3. In a small bowl, mix together the butter and olive oil and drizzle over the fish filets, flipping them to coat them fully.
4. Preheat the toaster oven to 350°F.
5. Place the fish in the air fryer oven and air-fry for 8 minutes, checking the fish for doneness after 4 minutes. The fish will flake easily when cooked.
6. Remove the fish from the air fryer oven. Top with chopped parsley and serve with lemon wedges.

Light Trout Amandine

Servings: 4
Cooking Time: 15 Minutes

Ingredients:
- 1 tablespoon margarine
- ½ cup sliced almonds
- 1 tablespoon lemon juice
- 1 teaspoon Worcestershire sauce
- Salt and freshly ground black pepper
- 4 6-ounce trout fillets
- 2 tablespoons chopped fresh parsley

Directions:
1. Combine the margarine and almonds in an oiled or nonstick 8½ × 8½ × 2-inch square baking (cake) pan.
2. BROIL for 5 minutes, or until the margarine is melted. Remove the pan from the oven and add the lemon juice and Worcestershire sauce. Season to taste with salt and pepper, and stir again to blend well. Add the trout fillets and spoon the mixture over them to coat well.
3. BROIL for 10 minutes, or until the almonds and fillets are lightly browned. Garnish with the chopped parsley before serving.

Oysters Broiled In Wine Sauce

Servings: 2
Cooking Time: 20 Minutes

Ingredients:
- Sauce:
- 2 tablespoons margarine, at room temperature
- 1 cup dry white wine
- 3 garlic cloves, minced
- Salt and freshly ground black pepper to taste
- 24 fresh oysters, shucked and drained

Directions:
1. Combine the sauce ingredients in a 1-quart 8½ × 8½ × 4-inch ovenproof baking dish and adjust the seasonings to taste.
2. BROIL the sauce for 5 minutes, remove the pan from the oven, and stir. Return to the oven and broil for another 5 minutes, or until the sauce begins to bubble. Remove from the oven and cool for 5 minutes. Add the oysters, spooning the sauce over them to cover thoroughly.
3. BROIL for 5 minutes, or until the oysters are just cooked.

Pecan-crusted Tilapia

Servings: 4
Cooking Time: 8 Minutes

Ingredients:
- 1 pound skinless, boneless tilapia filets
- ¼ cup butter, melted
- 1 teaspoon minced fresh or dried rosemary
- 1 cup finely chopped pecans
- 1 teaspoon sea salt
- ¼ teaspoon paprika
- 2 tablespoons chopped parsley
- 1 lemon, cut into wedges

Directions:
1. Pat the tilapia filets dry with paper towels.
2. Pour the melted butter over the filets and flip the filets to coat them completely.
3. In a medium bowl, mix together the rosemary, pecans, salt, and paprika.
4. Preheat the toaster oven to 350°F.
5. Place the tilapia filets into the air fryer oven and top with the pecan coating. Air-fry for 6 to 8 minutes. The fish should be firm to the touch and flake easily when fully cooked.
6. Remove the fish from the air fryer oven. Top the fish with chopped parsley and serve with lemon wedges.

Sesame-crusted Tuna Steaks

Servings: 3
Cooking Time: 13 Minutes

Ingredients:
- ½ cup Sesame seeds, preferably a blend of white and black
- 1½ tablespoons Toasted sesame oil
- 3 6-ounce skinless tuna steaks

Directions:
1. Preheat the toaster oven to 400°F.
2. Pour the sesame seeds on a dinner plate. Use ½ tablespoon of the sesame oil as a rub on both sides and the edges of a tuna steak. Set it in the sesame seeds, then turn it several times, pressing gently, to create an even coating of the seeds, including around the steak's edge. Set aside and continue coating the remaining steak(s).
3. When the machine is at temperature, set the steaks in the air fryer oven with as much air space between them as possible. Air-fry undisturbed for 10 minutes for medium-rare (not USDA-approved), or 12 to 13 minutes for cooked through (USDA-approved).
4. Use a nonstick-safe spatula to transfer the steaks to serving plates. Serve hot.

Quick Shrimp Scampi

Servings: 2
Cooking Time: 5 Minutes

Ingredients:
- 16 to 20 raw large shrimp, peeled, deveined and tails removed
- ½ cup white wine
- freshly ground black pepper
- ¼ cup + 1 tablespoon butter, divided
- 1 clove garlic, sliced
- 1 teaspoon olive oil
- salt, to taste
- juice of ½ lemon, to taste
- ¼ cup chopped fresh parsley

Directions:
1. Start by marinating the shrimp in the white wine and freshly ground black pepper for at least 30 minutes, or as long as 2 hours in the refrigerator.
2. Preheat the toaster oven to 400°F.
3. Melt ¼ cup of butter in a small saucepan on the stovetop. Add the garlic and let the butter simmer, but be sure to not let it burn.
4. Pour the shrimp and marinade into the air fryer oven, letting the marinade drain through to the bottom drawer. Drizzle the olive oil on the shrimp and season well with salt. Air-fry at 400°F for 3 minutes. Turn the shrimp over and pour the garlic butter over the shrimp. Air-fry for another 2 minutes.
5. Remove the shrimp from the air fryer oven and transfer them to a bowl. Squeeze lemon juice over all the shrimp and toss with the chopped parsley and remaining tablespoon of butter. Season to taste with salt and serve immediately.

Almond Crab Cakes

Servings: 4
Cooking Time: 10 Minutes

Ingredients:
- 1 pound cooked lump crabmeat, drained and picked over
- ¼ cup ground almonds
- 1 tablespoon Dijon mustard
- 1 scallion, white and green parts, finely chopped
- ½ red bell pepper, finely chopped
- 1 large egg
- 1 teaspoon lemon zest
- Oil spray (hand-pumped)
- 3 tablespoons almond flour

Directions:
1. Preheat the toaster oven to 375°F on AIR FRY for 5 minutes.
2. In a medium bowl, mix the crab meat, almonds, mustard, scallion, bell pepper, egg, and lemon zest until well combined and the mixture holds together when pressed. If the crab cakes do not stick together, add more ground almond.
3. Divide the crab mixture into 8 patties and press them to about 1 inch thick. Place them on a plate, cover, and chill for 30 minutes.
4. Place the air-fryer basket in the baking tray and generously spray with the oil.
5. Place the almond flour on a plate and dredge the crab cakes until they are lightly coated.
6. Place them in the basket and lightly spray both sides with the oil.
7. In position 2, air fry for 10 minutes, turning halfway through, until golden brown. Serve.

Crispy Pecan Fish

Servings: 4
Cooking Time: 20 Minutes

Ingredients:
- 3 tablespoons multigrain bread crumbs
- 3 tablespoons ground pecans
- 4 6-ounce fish fillets, approximately ¼ inch thick
- 1 egg white, whisked until frothy
- 1 tablespoon olive oil
- Salt and freshly ground black pepper to taste

Directions:
1. Combine the bread crumbs and pecans in a small bowl and transfer to a platter or plate.
2. Brush both sides of the fillets with egg white and dredge in the bread crumb/pecan mixture. Transfer the fillets to an oiled or nonstick 8½ × 8½ × 2-inch square baking (cake) pan.
3. BROIL for 10 minutes. Remove from the oven and carefully turn the fillets with a spatula. Broil again for 10 minutes, or until the fillets are lightly browned. Season to taste with the salt and pepper.

Coconut Shrimp

Servings: 4
Cooking Time: 15 Minutes

Ingredients:
- ¼ cup cassava flour
- 1 teaspoon sugar
- ¼ teaspoon black pepper
- ½ teaspoon salt
- 2 large eggs
- 1 cup shredded coconut flakes, unsweetened
- ½ pound deveined, tail-off large shrimp

Directions:
1. Preheat the toaster oven to 330°F. Spray the air fryer oven with olive oil spray. Set aside.
2. In a small bowl, mix the flour, sugar, pepper, and salt.
3. In a separate bowl, whisk the eggs.
4. In a third bowl, place the coconut flakes.
5. Place 1 shrimp at a time in the flour mixture, then wash with the eggs, and cover with coconut flakes.
6. Liberally spray the metal trivet that fits inside the air fryer oven with olive oil spray. Place the shrimp onto the metal trivet and air-fry for 15 minutes, flipping halfway through. Repeat until all shrimp are cooked.
7. Serve immediately with desired sauce.

Lemon-dill Salmon Burgers

Servings: 4
Cooking Time: 8 Minutes

Ingredients:
- 2 (6-ounce) fillets of salmon, finely chopped by hand or in a food processor
- 1 cup fine breadcrumbs
- 1 teaspoon freshly grated lemon zest
- 2 tablespoons chopped fresh dill weed
- 1 teaspoon salt
- freshly ground black pepper
- 2 eggs, lightly beaten
- 4 brioche or hamburger buns
- lettuce, tomato, red onion, avocado, mayonnaise or mustard, to serve

Directions:
1. Preheat the toaster oven to 400°F.
2. Combine all the ingredients in a bowl. Mix together well and divide into four balls. Flatten the balls into patties, making an indentation in the center of each patty with your thumb (this will help the burger stay flat as it cooks) and flattening the sides of the burgers so that they fit nicely into the air fryer oven.
3. Transfer the burgers to the air fryer oven and air-fry for 4 minutes. Flip the burgers over and air-fry for another 3 to 4 minutes, until nicely browned and firm to the touch.
4. Serve on soft brioche buns with your choice of topping – lettuce, tomato, red onion, avocado, mayonnaise or mustard.

Lemon-roasted Salmon Fillets

Servings: 3
Cooking Time: 7 Minutes

Ingredients:
- 3 6-ounce skin-on salmon fillets
- Olive oil spray
- 9 Very thin lemon slices
- ¾ teaspoon Ground black pepper
- ¼ teaspoon Table salt

Directions:
1. Preheat the toaster oven to 400°F.
2. Generously coat the skin of each of the fillets with olive oil spray. Set the fillets skin side down on your work surface. Place three overlapping lemon slices down the length of each salmon fillet. Sprinkle them with the pepper and salt. Coat lightly with olive oil spray.
3. Use a nonstick-safe spatula to transfer the fillets one by one to the air fryer oven, leaving as much air space between them as possible. Air-fry undisturbed for 7 minutes, or until cooked through.
4. Use a nonstick-safe spatula to transfer the fillets to serving plates. Cool for only a minute or two before serving.

DESSERTS

Frozen Brazo De Mercedes

Servings: 8
Cooking Time: 15 Minutes

Ingredients:
- 1 pint vanilla ice cream, softened to room temperature
- 1 (8 inch) premade graham cracker crust
- 6 large eggs, yolks and whites separated
- 7 ounces condensed milk
- ½ teaspoon vanilla extract
- ¼ teaspoon cream of tartar
- ⅓ cup granulated sugar

Directions:
1. Spread the ice cream on the bottom of the graham cracker crust in an even layer, cover with plastic wrap, and place in the freezer for 8 hours or overnight.
2. Whisk egg yolks and condensed milk over a double boiler continuously for 15 minutes or until the mixture becomes thick.
3. Whisk the vanilla extract into the egg mixture until fully combined.
4. Pass the custard through a fine sieve to remove any clumps.
5. Remove the ice cream and top with the egg yolk mixture, cover with plastic wrap, and place back into the freezer for 2 hours.
6. Beat the egg whites and cream of tartar in a stand mixer on high speed.
7. Add the sugar in slowly once the egg whites begin to foam.
8. Beat the egg whites for two minutes or until they form stiff peaks.
9. Remove the plastic wrap from the pie and top with the beaten egg whites.
10. Preheat the toaster Oven to 350°F.
11. Place the pie on the wire rack, then insert the rack at mid position in the preheated air fryer.
12. Select the Bake and Shake functions, adjust time to 15 minutes, and press Start/Pause.
13. Rotate the pie halfway through cooking for even browning. The Shake Reminder will let you know when.
14. Remove when done and place in the fridge for 1 hour, uncovered.
15. Cover the pie, then place in the freezer for 6 hours or overnight.
16. Remove the pie and allow it to rest at room temperature for 10 minutes, then slice and serve.

Orange-glazed Brownies

Servings: 12
Cooking Time: 30 Minutes

Ingredients:

- 3 squares unsweetened chocolate
- 3 tablespoons margarine
- 1 cup sugar
- ½ cup orange juice
- 2 eggs
- 1½ cups unbleached flour
- 1 teaspoon baking powder
- Salt to taste
- 1 tablespoon grated orange zest
- Orange Glaze (recipe follows)

Directions:

1. BROIL the chocolate and margarine in an oiled or nonstick 8½ × 8½ × 2-inch square baking (cake) pan for 3 minutes, or until almost melted. Remove from the oven and stir until completely melted. Transfer the chocolate/margarine mixture to a medium bowl.
2. Beat in the sugar, orange juice, and eggs with an electric mixer. Stir in the flour, baking powder, salt, and orange zest and mix until well blended. Pour into the oiled or nonstick square cake pan.
3. BAKE at 350° F. for 30 minutes, or until a toothpick inserted in the center comes out clean. Make holes over the entire top by piercing with a fork or toothpick. Paint with Orange Glaze and cut into squares.

Scones

Servings: 8
Cooking Time: 20 Minutes

Ingredients:
- Scone mixture:
- 1 cup unbleached flour
- 1 teaspoon baking powder
- 2 ¼ cup brown sugar
- 3 tablespoons vegetable oil
- 4 ¼ cup low-fat buttermilk
- 5 ½ teaspoon vanilla extract
- Topping mixture:
- 1 tablespoon granulated sugar
- 1 tablespoon margarine
- 1 teaspoon ground cinnamon

Directions:
1. Preheat the toaster oven to 425° F.
2. Combine the scone mixture ingredients in a medium bowl, cutting to blend with 2 butter knives or a pastry blender. Add a little more buttermilk, if necessary, so that the dough is moist enough to stay together when pinched.
3. KNEAD the dough on a lightly floured surface for 2 minutes, then place the dough in an oiled or nonstick 9¾-inch round cake pan and pat down to spread out evenly to the edges of the pan. Cut into 8 wedges.
4. Combine the topping mixture in a small bowl, mixing well, and sprinkle evenly on the dough.
5. BAKE for 20 minutes, or until golden brown.

Easy Churros

Servings: 12
Cooking Time: 10 Minutes

Ingredients:
- ½ cup Water
- 4 tablespoons (¼ cup/½ stick) Butter
- ¼ teaspoon Table salt
- ½ cup All-purpose flour
- 2 Large egg(s)
- ¼ cup Granulated white sugar
- 2 teaspoons Ground cinnamon

Directions:
1. Bring the water, butter, and salt to a boil in a small saucepan set over high heat, stirring occasionally.
2. When the butter has fully melted, reduce the heat to medium and stir in the flour to form a dough. Continue cooking, stirring constantly, to dry out the dough until it coats the bottom and sides of the pan with a film, even a crust. Remove the pan from the heat, scrape the dough into a bowl, and cool for 15 minutes.
3. Using an electric hand mixer at medium speed, beat in the egg, or eggs one at a time, until the dough is smooth and firm enough to hold its shape.
4. Mix the sugar and cinnamon in a small bowl. Scoop up 1 tablespoon of the dough and roll it in the sugar mixture to form a small, coated tube about ½ inch in diameter and 2 inches long. Set it aside and make 5 more tubes for the small batch or 11 more for the large one.
5. Set the tubes on a plate and freeze for 20 minutes. Meanwhile, preheat the toaster oven to 375°F.
6. Set 3 frozen tubes in the air fryer oven for a small batch or 6 for a large one with as much air space between them as possible. Air-fry undisturbed for 10 minutes, or until puffed, brown, and set.
7. Use kitchen tongs to transfer the churros to a wire rack to cool for at least 5 minutes. Meanwhile, air-fry and cool the second batch of churros in the same way.

Bourbon Bread Pudding

Servings: 2
Cooking Time: 120 Minutes

Ingredients:
- 6 ounces baguette, torn into 1-inch pieces (4 cups)
- ¼ cup raisins
- 2 tablespoons bourbon
- ¾ cup heavy cream
- ⅓ cup packed (2⅓ ounces) light brown sugar
- ¼ cup whole milk
- 2 large egg yolks
- 1 teaspoon vanilla extract
- ½ teaspoon ground cinnamon, divided
- ⅛ teaspoon table salt
- Pinch ground nutmeg
- 2 tablespoons unsalted butter, cut into ¼-inch pieces
- 1 tablespoon granulated sugar

Directions:
1. Adjust toaster oven rack to middle position and preheat the toaster oven to 375 degrees. Spread bread in single layer on small rimmed baking sheet and bake until golden brown and crisp, 10 to 20 minutes, tossing halfway through baking. Let bread cool completely.
2. Meanwhile, microwave raisins and bourbon in covered bowl until bubbling, 30 to 60 seconds. Let sit until softened, about 15 minutes.
3. Whisk cream, brown sugar, milk, egg yolks, vanilla, ¼ teaspoon cinnamon, salt, and nutmeg together in large bowl. Add bread and raisin mixture and toss until evenly coated. Let mixture sit, tossing occasionally, until bread begins to absorb custard and is softened, about 20 minutes.
4. Grease two 12-ounce ramekins. Divide bread mixture evenly between prepared ramekins and sprinkle with butter, granulated sugar, and remaining ¼ teaspoon cinnamon. Cover each ramekin with aluminum foil, place on small rimmed baking sheet, and bake for 30 minutes.
5. Remove foil from bread puddings and continue to bake until tops are crisp and golden brown, 10 to 15 minutes. Let bread puddings cool for 15 minutes before serving.

Blueberry Crumbles

Servings: 2
Cooking Time: 60 Minutes

Ingredients:
- 2 tablespoons granulated sugar
- 1½ teaspoons cornstarch
- ⅛ teaspoon table salt, divided
- 10 ounces (2 cups) blueberries
- ½ cup (1½ ounces) old-fashioned rolled oats
- ¼ cup (1¼ ounces) all-purpose flour
- ¼ cup packed (1¾ ounces) light brown sugar
- ¼ teaspoon ground cinnamon
- 4 tablespoons unsalted butter, melted and cooled

Directions:
1. Adjust toaster oven rack to lowest position and preheat the toaster oven to 375 degrees. Combine granulated sugar, cornstarch, and pinch salt in medium bowl. Gently toss blueberries in sugar mixture, then divide between two 12-ounce ramekins.
2. Combine oats, flour, brown sugar, cinnamon, and remaining pinch salt in now-empty bowl. Drizzle with melted butter and toss with fork until evenly moistened and mixture forms large chunks with some pea-size pieces throughout. Sprinkle topping evenly over blueberries, breaking up any large chunks.
3. Place ramekins on aluminum foil–lined small rimmed baking sheet and bake until filling is bubbling around edges and topping is deep golden brown, 25 to 30 minutes, rotating sheet halfway through baking. Let crumbles cool on wire rack for 15 minutes before serving.

Chocolate Cupcakes With Salted Caramel Buttercream

Servings: 12
Cooking Time: 20 Minutes

Ingredients:
- Cake Ingredients
- 1 egg
- ½ cup vegetable oil
- ½ cup buttermilk
- ½ teaspoon vanilla extract
- 1 cup granulated sugar
- 1 cup all-purpose flour
- ¼ cup dark cocoa powder
- 1 teaspoon baking soda
- ½ teaspoon salt
- ½ teaspoon instant espresso powder
- ½ cup boiling water (205°-212°F)
- Buttercream Ingredients
- ½ cup unsalted butter, room temperature
- ⅓ cup caramel sauce, room temperature
- ½ teaspoon vanilla extract
- ½ teaspoon kosher salt
- 1 cup powdered sugar

Directions:
1. Whisk together the egg, vegetable oil, buttermilk, and vanilla extract in a bowl and set aside.
2. Sift together sugar, flour, cocoa powder, baking soda, salt, and instant espresso in a large mixing bowl.
3. Add the wet ingredients into the dry and mix until well combined.
4. Pour in the boiling water slowly while whisking vigorously until the batter is smooth.
5. Line the muffin pan with cupcake liners, then pour in the batter.
6. Preheat the toaster Oven to 350°F.
7. Place the cupcakes on the wire rack, then insert the rack at mid position in the preheated oven.
8. Select the Bake and Fan functions, adjust time to 20 minutes, and press Start/Pause.
9. Remove when done and allow cupcakes to cool on a wire rack for 2 hours.
10. Beat butter using a stand mixer on medium speed for 1 minute or until smooth and fluffy.
11. Beat in the caramel sauce, vanilla, and salt for 2 minutes or until well combined. You may need to scrape down the side of the bowl occasionally.
12. Add the powdered sugar slowly, beating on low speed until fully incorporated.
13. Beat the buttercream on medium speed for 2 minutes or until smooth and creamy.
14. Pipe the buttercream onto the cooled cupcake using a decorated tip.
15. Place the cakes in the fridge for 30 minutes before serving.

Baked Custard

Servings: 2
Cooking Time: 45 Minutes

Ingredients:
- 2 eggs
- ¼ cup sugar
- 1 cup low-fat evaporated milk
- ½ teaspoon vanilla extract
- Pinch of grated nutmeg
- Fat-free half-and-half

Directions:
1. Preheat the toaster oven to 350° F.
2. Beat together the eggs, sugar, milk, vanilla, and nutmeg in a small bowl with an electric mixer at medium speed. Pour equal portions of the custard mixture into 2 oiled 1-cup-size ovenproof dishes.
3. BAKE for 45 minutes, or until a toothpick inserted in the center comes out clean. Serve drizzled with warm fat-free half-and-half.

Not Key Lime, Lime Pie

Servings: 3
Cooking Time: 27 Minutes

Ingredients:
- 1 tablespoon grated lime zest
- 3 large egg yolks
- 1 (14-ounce) can sweetened condensed milk
- ½ cup fresh lime juice
- 1 ¾ cups graham cracker crumbs (about 12 full graham crackers)
- ⅓ cup granulated sugar
- ⅛ teaspoon table salt
- ½ cup unsalted butter, melted
- Nonstick cooking spray
- WHIPPED CREAM
- 1 cup heavy cream
- ⅓ cup confectioners' sugar

Directions:
1. Preheat the toaster oven to 350°F.
2. Whisk the lime zest and egg yolks in a large bowl for 1 minute. Whisk in the sweetened condensed milk and lime juice. Set aside to thicken while you prepare the crust.
3. Stir the graham cracker crumbs, granulated sugar, and salt in a medium bowl. Pour the butter over the mixture and mix until combined and moist. Press the crust evenly into the bottom and up the sides of a 9-inch pie plate. Pack tightly using the back of a large spoon. Bake for 10 minutes. Let cool on a cooling rack.
4. When the crust is completely cool, pour the lime filling inside. Bake for 15 to 17 minutes, or until the center is set (it will still jiggle a bit). Allow the pie to cool completely at room temperature. Spray plastic wrap with nonstick cooking spray and place on the pie. Refrigerate for at least 3 hours or overnight.
5. Beat the cream in a large bowl with an electric mixer at medium-high speed until soft peaks form. Add the confectioners' sugar, one tablespoon at a time, and continue to beat until stiff peaks form. Dollop, pipe, or spread the whipped cream over the pie before serving. Refrigerate leftovers for up to 3 days.

Easy Peach Turnovers

Servings: 6
Cooking Time: 35 Minutes

Ingredients:
- 1 ½ tablespoons granulated sugar
- 1 teaspoon cornstarch
- ¾ cup chopped peeled peaches, fresh or frozen and thawed
- ½ teaspoon grated lemon zest
- ⅛ teaspoon ground nutmeg
- Dash table salt
- 1 sheet frozen puff pastry, about 9 inches square, thawed (½ of a 17.3-ounce package)
- 1 large egg
- Coarse white sugar
- GLAZE
- ¾ cup confectioners' sugar
- ½ teaspoon pure vanilla extract
- 1 to 2 tablespoons milk

Directions:
1. Line a 12 x 12-inch baking pan with parchment paper.
2. Stir the granulated sugar and cornstarch in a medium bowl. Stir in the peaches, lemon zest, nutmeg, and salt. Mix until the sugar-cornstarch mixture coats the peaches evenly and the sugar begins to dissolve; set aside.
3. On a lightly floured board, roll the puff pastry sheet into a 13 ½ x 9-inch rectangle. Cut the puff pastry into 6 (4 ½-inch) squares. Lightly beat the egg in a small bowl, then brush the edges of each puff pastry square with the egg. Reserve the remaining egg to brush on top of each turnover.
4. Spoon about 2 tablespoons peach mixture into the center of each square. Fold the pastry over the peaches to form a triangle, pinching to seal the edges. Using the tines of a fork, crimp the edges tightly. Lightly brush the top of each turnover with the egg. Sprinkle each with the coarse sugar.
5. Place the turnovers on the prepared pan. Freeze the turnovers for 15 minutes.
6. Preheat the toaster oven to 375°F. Bake for 15 to 20 minutes or until golden brown. Let cool 5 to 10 minutes.
7. Meanwhile make the glaze: Whisk the confectioners' sugar, vanilla, and 1 tablespoon milk in a small bowl until smooth. If needed, stir in the additional milk to reach the desired consistency. Drizzle the glaze from the tip of a teaspoon in decorative stripes over the turnovers.

Chewy Coconut Cake

Servings: 6
Cooking Time: 22 Minutes

Ingredients:
- ¾ cup plus 2½ tablespoons All-purpose flour
- ¾ teaspoon Baking powder
- ⅛ teaspoon Table salt
- 7½ tablespoons (1 stick minus ½ tablespoon) Butter, at room temperature
- ⅓ cup plus 1 tablespoon Granulated white sugar
- 5 tablespoons Packed light brown sugar
- 5 tablespoons Pasteurized egg substitute, such as Egg Beaters
- 2 teaspoons Vanilla extract
- ½ cup Unsweetened shredded coconut
- Baking spray

Directions:
1. Preheat the toaster oven to 325°F.
2. Mix the flour, baking powder, and salt in a small bowl until well combined.
3. Using an electric hand mixer at medium speed, beat the butter, granulated white sugar, and brown sugar in a medium bowl until creamy and smooth, about 3 minutes, occasionally scraping down the inside of the bowl. Beat in the egg substitute or egg and vanilla until smooth.
4. Scrape down and remove the beaters. Fold in the flour mixture with a rubber spatula just until all the flour is moistened. Fold in the coconut until the mixture is a uniform color.
5. Use the baking spray to generously coat the inside of a 6-inch round cake pan for a small batch, a 7-inch round cake pan for a medium batch, or an 8-inch round cake pan for a large batch. Scrape and spread the batter into the pan, smoothing the batter out to an even layer.
6. Set the pan in the toaster oven and air-fry for 18 minutes for a 6-inch layer, 20 minutes for a 7-inch layer, or 22 minutes for an 8-inch layer, or until the cake is well browned and set even if there's a little soft give right at the center. Start checking it at the 16-minute mark to know where you are.
7. Use hot pads or silicone baking mitts to transfer the cake pan to a wire rack. Cool for at least 1 hour or up to 4 hours. Use a nonstick-safe knife to slice the cake into wedges right in the pan, lifting them out one by one.

Blackberry Pie

Servings: 6
Cooking Time: 30 Minutes

Ingredients:
- Filling:
- 2 16-ounce bags frozen blackberries, thawed, or 2 cups fresh blackberries, washed and well drained
- 1 4-ounce jar baby food prunes
- 2 tablespoons cornstarch
- 3 ¼ cup brown sugar
- 1 tablespoon lemon juice
- Salt to taste
- 1 Graham Cracker Crust, baked (recipe follows)
- Meringue Topping (recipe follows)

Directions:
1. Preheat the toaster oven to 350° F.
2. Combine the filling ingredients in a large bowl, mixing well. Spoon the filling into the baked Graham Cracker Crust and spread evenly.
3. BAKE for 30 minutes. When cool, top with the Meringue Topping.

BREAKFAST

Green Onion Pancakes

Servings: 4
Cooking Time: 8 Minutes

Ingredients:
- 2 cup all-purpose flour
- ½ teaspoon salt
- ¾ cup hot water
- 1 tablespoon vegetable oil
- 1 tablespoon butter, melted
- 2 cups finely chopped green onions
- 1 tablespoon black sesame seeds, for garnish

Directions:
1. In a large bowl, whisk together the flour and salt. Make a well in the center and pour in the hot water. Quickly stir the flour mixture together until a dough forms. Knead the dough for 5 minutes; then cover with a warm, wet towel and set aside for 30 minutes to rest.
2. In a small bowl, mix together the vegetable oil and melted butter.
3. On a floured surface, place the dough and cut it into 8 pieces. Working with 1 piece of dough at a time, use a rolling pin to roll out the dough until it's ¼ inch thick; then brush the surface with the oil and butter mixture and sprinkle with green onions. Next, fold the dough in half and then in half again. Roll out the dough again until it's ¼ inch thick and brush with the oil and butter mixture and green onions. Fold the dough in half and then in half again and roll out one last time until it's ¼ inch thick. Repeat this technique with all 8 pieces.
4. Meanwhile, preheat the toaster oven to 400°F.
5. Place 1 or 2 pancakes into the air fryer oven (or as many as will fit in your fryer), and air-fry for 2 minutes or until crispy and golden brown. Repeat until all the pancakes are cooked. Top with black sesame seeds for garnish, if desired.

Yogurt Bread

Servings: 2
Cooking Time: 40 Minutes

Ingredients:
- 3 cups unbleached flour
- 4 teaspoons baking powder
- 5 2 teaspoons sugar
- Salt to taste
- 1 cup plain nonfat yogurt
- ¼ cup vegetable oil
- 1 egg, beaten, to brush the top

Directions:
1. Preheat the toaster oven to 375° F.
2. Combine the flour, baking powder, sugar, and salt in a large bowl. Make a hole in the center and spoon in the yogurt and oil.
3. Stir the flour into the center. When the dough is well mixed, turn it out onto a lightly floured surface and knead for 8 minutes, until the dough is smooth and elastic. Place the dough in an oiled or nonstick regular-size 8½ × 4½ × 2¼-inch loaf pan. Brush the top with the beaten egg.
4. BAKE for 40 minutes, or until a toothpick inserted in the center comes out clean and the loaf is browned. Invert on a wire rack to cool.

Lemon Blueberry Scones

Servings: 6
Cooking Time: 25 Minutes

Ingredients:
- 1 ½ cups all-purpose flour
- 2 tablespoons granulated sugar
- 2 ¼ teaspoons baking powder
- 1 teaspoon grated lemon zest
- ¼ teaspoon table salt
- ¼ cup unsalted butter, cut into 1-tablespoon pieces
- ¾ cup fresh or frozen blueberries
- ¾ cup plus 1 tablespoon heavy cream, plus more for brushing
- Coarse white sugar
- LEMON GLAZE
- 1 cup confectioners' sugar
- 2 to 3 tablespoons fresh lemon juice

Directions:
1. Line a 12 x 12-inch baking pan with parchment paper.
2. Whisk the flour, granulated sugar, baking powder, lemon zest, and salt in a large bowl. Cut in the butter using a pastry cutter or two knives until the mixture is crumbly throughout. Gently stir in the blueberries, taking care not to mash them. Add ¾ cup cream and gently stir until a soft dough forms. If needed, stir in an additional tablespoon of cream so all of the flour is moistened.
3. Turn the dough onto a lightly floured board. Pat the dough into a circle about ¾ inch thick and 6 inches in diameter. Cut into 6 triangles. Arrange the triangles on the prepared pan. Freeze for 15 minutes.
4. Preheat the toaster oven to 400°F. Brush the scones lightly with cream and sprinkle with coarse sugar. Bake for 20 to 25 minutes or until golden brown. Let cool for 5 minutes.
5. Meanwhile, make the glaze: Stir the confectioners' sugar and lemon juice in a small bowl, blending until smooth. Drizzle the glaze over the scones. Let stand for about 5 minutes. These taste best served freshly made and slightly warm.

Chocolate Chip Banana Muffins

Servings: 12
Cooking Time: 14 Minutes

Ingredients:
- 2 medium bananas, mashed
- ¼ cup brown sugar
- 1½ teaspoons vanilla extract
- ⅔ cup milk
- 2 tablespoons butter
- 1 large egg
- 1 cup white whole-wheat flour
- ½ cup old-fashioned oats
- 1 teaspoon baking soda
- ½ teaspoon baking powder
- ⅛ teaspoon sea salt
- ¼ cup mini chocolate chips

Directions:
1. Preheat the toaster oven to 330°F.
2. In a large bowl, combine the bananas, brown sugar, vanilla extract, milk, butter, and egg; set aside.
3. In a separate bowl, combine the flour, oats, baking soda, baking powder, and salt.
4. Slowly add the dry ingredients into the wet ingredients, folding in the flour mixture ⅓ cup at a time.
5. Mix in the chocolate chips and set aside.
6. Using silicone muffin liners, fill 6 muffin liners two-thirds full. Carefully place the muffin liners in the air fryer oven and bake for 20 minutes (or until the tops are browned and a toothpick inserted in the center comes out clean). Carefully remove the muffins from the air fryer oven and repeat with the remaining batter.
7. Serve warm.

Cinnamon Toast

Servings: 2
Cooking Time: 2 Minutes

Ingredients:
- 1 tablespoon brown sugar
- 2 teaspoons margarine, at room temperature
- ¼ teaspoon ground cinnamon
- 2 slices whole wheat or multigrain bread

Directions:
1. Combine the sugar, margarine, and cinnamon in a small bowl with a fork until well blended. Spread each bread slice with equal portions of the mixture.
2. TOAST once, or until the sugar is melted and the bread is browned to your preference.

Popovers

Servings: 6
Cooking Time: 30 Minutes

Ingredients:
- 2 eggs
- 1 cup skim milk
- 2 tablespoons vegetable oil
- 1 cup unbleached flour
- Salt to taste

Directions:
1. Preheat the toaster oven to 400° F.
2. Beat all the ingredients in a medium bowl with an electric mixer at high speed until smooth. The batter should be the consistency of heavy cream.
3. Fill the pans of a 6-muffin tin three-quarters full.
4. BAKE for 20 minutes, then reduce the heat to 350° F. and bake for 10 minutes, or until golden brown.

Coffee Cake

Servings: 6
Cooking Time: 40 Minutes

Ingredients:
- Cake:
- 2 cups unbleached flour
- 2 teaspoons baking powder
- 2 tablespoons vegetable oil
- 1 egg
- 1¼ cups skim milk
- Topping:
- ½ cup brown sugar
- 1 tablespoon margarine, at room temperature
- 1 teaspoon ground cinnamon
- ¼ teaspoon grated nutmeg
- ¼ cup chopped pecans
- Salt to taste

Directions:
1. Preheat the toaster oven to 375° F.
2. Combine the ingredients for the cake in a medium bowl and mix thoroughly. Pour the batter into an oiled or 8½ × 8½ × 2inch square baking (cake) pan and set aside.
3. Combine the topping ingredients in a small bowl, mashing the margarine into the dry ingredients with a fork until the mixture is crumbly. Sprinkle evenly on top of the batter.
4. BAKE for 40 minutes, or until a toothpick inserted in the center comes out clean. Cool and cut into squares.

Spinach, Tomato & Feta Quiche

Servings: 8
Cooking Time: 60 Minutes

Ingredients:
- Pie Crust Ingredients
- 1½ cups all-purpose flour, plus more for dusting
- ½ teaspoon kosher salt
- 3 tablespoons unsalted butter, chilled and cubed
- 6 tablespoons vegetable shortening, chilled
- 3 tablespoons ice water
- Dry beans or uncooked rice, for filling
- Filling Ingredients
- 1½ ounces frozen spinach, thawed and squeezed dry
- 9 cherry tomatoes, halved
- 1½ ounces crumbled feta cheese 4 large eggs
- ½ cup heavy cream
- ½ teaspoon kosher salt
- ¼ teaspoon freshly ground black pepper
- Extra virgin olive oil, for drizzling

Directions:
1. Combine the flour and salt in a food processor and pulse once to combine.
2. Add the butter and shortening, then pulse until the mixture creates fine crumbs.
3. Pour the water in slowly and pulse until it forms a dough.
4. Form the dough into a square, wrap with plastic wrap, and place in the fridge for 6 hours or overnight.
5. Remove the dough from the fridge, unwrap it, and place onto a lightly floured work surface.
6. Roll out the dough into a 10-inch diameter circle. You may need to use additional flour to keep the dough from sticking to the rolling pin.
7. Place the dough into the tart pan and use your fingers to form the dough to fit the pan.
8. Trim the edges and prick the bottom of the tart shell all over.
9. Cover with plastic wrap and place in the freezer for 30 minutes.
10. Remove from the freezer, unwrap, and top with parchment paper that covers all the edges.
11. Fill the tart shell with dry beans or uncooked rice until the dough is fully covered. Set aside.
12. Preheat the toaster Oven to 350°F.
13. Place the tart shell on the wire rack, then insert the rack at low position in the preheated oven.
14. Select the Bake function, press the Fan/Light button to start the fan, then press Start/Pause.
15. Remove the tart shell from the oven and let it cool for 1 hour.
16. Arrange the spinach, tomatoes, and feta cheese evenly inside the empty tart shell.
17. Whisk together the eggs, heavy cream, salt, and pepper until well combined.
18. Pour the egg mixture into the filled tart shell and lightly drizzle with extra-virgin olive oil. You may have some extra filling left over.
19. Preheat the toaster Oven to 350°F.
20. Place the quiche on the wire rack, then insert the rack at low position in the preheated oven.
21. Select the Bake function, then press Start/Pause.
22. Remove the quiche from the oven and let it cool for 5 minutes.
23. Cut into slices and serve.

Flaky Granola

Servings: 3
Cooking Time: 20 Minutes

Ingredients:
- ¼ cup rolled oats
- ½ cup wheat flakes
- ½ cup bran flakes
- ¼ cup wheat germ
- 3 tablespoons sesame seeds
- 4 ¼ cup unsweetened shredded coconut
- ½ cup chopped almonds, walnuts, or pecans
- 2 tablespoons chopped pumpkin seeds
- ½ cup honey or molasses
- 2 tablespoons vegetable oil
- Salt to taste

Directions:
1. Preheat the toaster oven to 375° F.
2. Combine all the ingredients in a medium bowl, stirring to mix well.
3. Spread the mixture in an oiled or nonstick 6½ × 6½ × 2-inch square (cake) pan.
4. BAKE for 20 minutes, turning with tongs every 5 minutes to toast evenly. Cool and store in an airtight container in the refrigerator.

Strawberry Pie

Servings: 6
Cooking Time: 25 Minutes

Ingredients:
- 2 16-ounce packages frozen sliced strawberries or 1 quart fresh strawberries, washed, stemmed, and sliced
- ¼ cup sugar
- 2 tablespoons lemon juice
- 2 tablespoons cornstarch
- 1 single Oatmeal Piecrust, baked (recipe follows)
- Strawberry Pie Glaze (recipe follows)

Directions:
1. Preheat the toaster oven to 350° F.
2. Combine the strawberries, sugar, lemon juice, and cornstarch in a medium bowl, mixing well. Fill the piecrust shell with the strawberries, spreading evenly.
3. BAKE for 25 minutes, or until the strawberries are tender. Glaze with Strawberry Pie Glaze.

Yogurt Cheese Spread

Servings: 1
Cooking Time: 5 Minutes

Ingredients:
- 1 cup plain yogurt (without starch, gum, or gelatin added)
- Seasonings:
- 1 tablespoon olive oil
- 1 teaspoon chopped fresh chives
- Salt and butcher's pepper or freshly ground black pepper to taste

Directions:
1. Place 2 coffee filters in a sieve over a bowl. Spoon the yogurt into the filters and place in the refrigerator for 6 to 8 hours, or until most of the moisture is drained from the yogurt and it is firm. Changing coffee filters several times during draining will expedite the process. Transfer the yogurt cheese to a bowl and add the oil, chives, and seasonings. Blend well and adjust the seasonings to taste.

Walnut Pancake

Servings: 4
Cooking Time: 20 Minutes

Ingredients:
- 3 tablespoons butter, divided into thirds
- 1 cup flour
- 1½ teaspoons baking powder
- ¼ teaspoon salt
- 2 tablespoons sugar
- ¾ cup milk
- 1 egg, beaten
- 1 teaspoon pure vanilla extract
- ½ cup walnuts, roughly chopped
- maple syrup or fresh sliced fruit, for serving

Directions:
1. Place 1 tablespoon of the butter in air fryer oven baking pan. Air-fry at 330°F for 3 minutes to melt.
2. In a small dish or pan, melt the remaining 2 tablespoons of butter either in the microwave or on the stove.
3. In a medium bowl, stir together the flour, baking powder, salt, and sugar. Add milk, beaten egg, the 2 tablespoons of melted butter, and vanilla. Stir until combined but do not beat. Batter may be slightly lumpy.
4. Pour batter over the melted butter in air fryer oven baking pan. Sprinkle nuts evenly over top.
5. Air-fry for 20 minutes or until toothpick inserted in center comes out clean. Turn air fryer oven off, close the machine, and let pancake rest for 2 minutes.
6. Remove pancake from pan, slice, and serve with syrup or fresh fruit.

BEEF PORK AND LAMB

Crispy Lamb Shoulder Chops

Servings: 3
Cooking Time: 28 Minutes

Ingredients:
- ¾ cup All-purpose flour or gluten-free all-purpose flour
- 2 teaspoons Mild paprika
- 2 teaspoons Table salt
- 1½ teaspoons Garlic powder
- 1½ teaspoons Dried sage leaves
- 3 6-ounce bone-in lamb shoulder chops, any excess fat trimmed
- Olive oil spray

Directions:
1. Whisk the flour, paprika, salt, garlic powder, and sage in a large bowl until the mixture is of a uniform color. Add the chops and toss well to coat. Transfer them to a cutting board.
2. Preheat the toaster oven to 375°F.
3. When the machine is at temperature, again dredge the chops one by one in the flour mixture. Lightly coat both sides of each chop with olive oil spray before putting it in the air fryer oven. Continue on with the remaining chop(s), leaving air space between them in the air fryer oven.
4. Air-fry, turning once, for 25 minutes, or until the chops are well browned and tender when pierced with the point of a paring knife. If the machine is at 360°F, you may need to add up to 3 minutes to the cooking time.
5. Use kitchen tongs to transfer the chops to a wire rack. Cool for 5 minutes before serving.

California Burritos

Servings: 4
Cooking Time: 17 Minutes

Ingredients:
- 1 pound sirloin steak, sliced thin
- 1 teaspoon dried oregano
- 1 teaspoon ground cumin
- ½ teaspoon garlic powder
- 16 tater tots
- ⅓ cup sour cream
- ½ lime, juiced
- 2 tablespoons hot sauce
- 1 large avocado, pitted
- 1 teaspoon salt, divided
- 4 large (8- to 10-inch) flour tortillas
- ½ cup shredded cheddar cheese or Monterey jack
- 2 tablespoons avocado oil

Directions:
1. Preheat the toaster oven to 380°F.
2. Season the steak with oregano, cumin, and garlic powder. Place the steak on one side of the air fryer oven and the tater tots on the other side. (It's okay for them to touch, because the flavors will all come together in the burrito.) Air-fry for 8 minutes, toss, and cook an additional 4 to 6 minutes.
3. Meanwhile, in a small bowl, stir together the sour cream, lime juice, and hot sauce.
4. In another small bowl, mash together the avocado and season with ½ teaspoon of the salt, to taste.
5. To assemble the burrito, lay out the tortillas, equally divide the meat amongst the tortillas. Season the steak equally with the remaining ½ teaspoon salt. Then layer the mashed avocado and sour cream mixture on top. Top each tortilla with 4 tater tots and finish each with 2 tablespoons cheese. Roll up the sides and, while holding in the sides, roll up the burrito. Place the burritos in the air fryer oven and brush with avocado oil (working in batches as needed); air-fry for 3 minutes or until lightly golden on the outside.

Slow Cooked Carnitas

Servings: 6
Cooking Time: 360 Minutes

Ingredients:
- 1 pork shoulder (5 pounds), bone-in
- 2½ teaspoons kosher salt
- 1½ teaspoons black pepper
- 1½ teaspoons ground cumin
- 1 teaspoon dried oregano
- ¼ teaspoon ground coriander
- 2 bay leaves
- 6 garlic cloves
- 1 small onion, quartered
- 1 cinnamon stick
- 1 full orange peel (no white)
- 2 oranges, juiced
- 1 lime, juiced

Directions:
1. Season the pork shoulder with salt, pepper, cumin, oregano, and coriander.
2. Place the seasoned pork shoulder in a large pot along with any seasoning that did not stick to the pork.
3. Add in the bay leaves, garlic cloves, onion, cinnamon stick, and orange peel.
4. Squeeze in the juice of two oranges and one lime and cover with foil.
5. Insert the wire rack at low position in the Air Fryer Toaster Oven, then place the pot on the rack.
6. Select the Slow Cook function and press Start/Pause.
7. Remove carefully when done, uncover, and remove the bone.
8. Shred the carnitas and use them in tacos, burritos, or any other way you please.

Beef Vegetable Stew

Servings: 4
Cooking Time: 120 Minutes

Ingredients:
- 1 pound lean stewing beef, cut into 1-inch chunks
- 2 carrots, diced
- 2 celery stalks
- 1 large potato, diced
- ½ sweet onion, chopped
- 2 teaspoons minced garlic
- 1 (15-ounce) can diced tomatoes, with juices
- 1 teaspoon sea salt
- ½ teaspoon freshly ground black pepper
- 1 cup low-sodium beef broth
- 3 tablespoons all-purpose flour
- 1 cup frozen peas

Directions:
1. Place the rack in position 1 and preheat the toaster oven to 375°F on BAKE for 5 minutes.
2. In a 1½-quart casserole dish, combine the beef, carrots, celery, potato, onion, garlic, tomatoes, salt, and pepper.
3. In a small bowl, stir the broth and flour until well combined. Add the broth mixture to the beef mixture and stir to combine.
4. Cover with foil or a lid and bake for 2 hours, stirring each time you reset the timer, until the meat is very tender.
5. Stir in the peas and let stand for 10 minutes. Serve.

Smokehouse-style Beef Ribs

Servings: 3
Cooking Time: 25 Minutes

Ingredients:
- ¼ teaspoon Mild smoked paprika
- ¼ teaspoon Garlic powder
- ¼ teaspoon Onion powder
- ¼ teaspoon Table salt
- ¼ teaspoon Ground black pepper
- 3 10- to 12-ounce beef back ribs (not beef short ribs)

Directions:
1. Preheat the toaster oven to 350°F.
2. Mix the smoked paprika, garlic powder, onion powder, salt, and pepper in a small bowl until uniform. Massage and pat this mixture onto the ribs.
3. When the machine is at temperature, set the ribs in the air fryer oven in one layer, turning them on their sides if necessary, sort of like they're spooning but with at least ¼ inch air space between them. Air-fry for 25 minutes, turning once, until deep brown and sizzling.
4. Use kitchen tongs to transfer the ribs to a wire rack. Cool for 5 minutes before serving.

Chicken Fried Steak

Servings: 4
Cooking Time: 15 Minutes

Ingredients:
- 2 eggs
- ½ cup buttermilk
- 1½ cups flour
- ¾ teaspoon salt
- ½ teaspoon pepper
- 1 pound beef cube steaks
- salt and pepper
- oil for misting or cooking spray

Directions:
1. Beat together eggs and buttermilk in a shallow dish.
2. In another shallow dish, stir together the flour, ½ teaspoon salt, and ¼ teaspoon pepper.
3. Season cube steaks with remaining salt and pepper to taste. Dip in flour, buttermilk egg wash, and then flour again.
4. Spray both sides of steaks with oil or cooking spray.
5. Cooking in 2 batches, place steaks in air fryer oven in single layer. Air-fry at 360°F for 10 minutes. Spray tops of steaks with oil and cook 5 minutes or until meat is well done.
6. Repeat to cook remaining steaks.

Lamb Curry

Servings: 4
Cooking Time: 40 Minutes

Ingredients:
- 1 pound lean lamb for stewing, trimmed and cut into 1 × 1-inch pieces
- 1 small onion, chopped
- 3 garlic cloves, minced
- 2 plum tomatoes, chopped
- ½ cup dry white wine
- 2 tablespoons curry powder
- Salt and cayenne to taste

Directions:
1. Preheat the toaster oven to 400° F.
2. Combine all the ingredients in an 8½ × 8½ × 4-inch ovenproof baking dish. Adjust the seasonings.
3. BAKE, covered, for 40 minutes, or until the meat is tender and the onion is cooked.

Beer-baked Pork Tenderloin

Servings: 4
Cooking Time: 40 Minutes

Ingredients:
- 1 pound lean pork tenderloin, fat trimmed off
- 3 garlic cloves, minced
- 1 cup good-quality dark ale or beer
- 2 bay leaves
- Salt and freshly cracked black pepper
- Spiced apple slices

Directions:
1. Preheat the toaster oven to 400° F.
2. Place the tenderloin in an 8½ × 8½ × 4-inch ovenproof baking dish. Sprinkle the minced garlic over the pork, pour over the beer, add the bay leaves, and season to taste with the salt and pepper. Cover with aluminum foil.
3. BAKE, covered, for 40 minutes, or until the meat is tender. Discard the bay leaves and serve sliced with the liquid. Garnish with the spiced apple slices.

Crispy Smoked Pork Chops

Servings: 3
Cooking Time: 8 Minutes

Ingredients:
- ⅔ cup All-purpose flour or tapioca flour
- 1 Large egg white(s)
- 2 tablespoons Water
- 1½ cups Corn flake crumbs (gluten-free, if a concern)
- 3 ½-pound, ½-inch-thick bone-in smoked pork chops

Directions:
1. Preheat the toaster oven to 375°F.
2. Set up and fill three shallow soup plates or small pie plates on your counter: one for the flour; one for the egg white(s), whisked with the water until foamy; and one for the corn flake crumbs.
3. Set a chop in the flour and turn it several times, coating both sides and the edges. Gently shake off any excess flour, then set it in the beaten egg white mixture. Turn to coat both sides as well as the edges. Let any excess egg white slip back into the rest, then set the chop in the corn flake crumbs. Turn it several times, pressing gently to coat the chop evenly on both sides and around the edge. Set the chop aside and continue coating the remaining chop(s) in the same way.
4. Set the chops in the air fryer oven with as much air space between them as possible. Air-fry undisturbed for 8 minutes, or until the coating is crunchy and the chops are heated through.
5. Use kitchen tongs to transfer the chops to a wire rack and cool for a couple of minutes before serving.

Bourbon Broiled Steak

Servings: 2
Cooking Time: 14 Minutes

Ingredients:
- Brushing mixture:
- ¼ cup bourbon
- 1 teaspoon garlic powder
- 1 tablespoon olive oil
- 1 teaspoon soy sauce
- 2 6- to 8-ounce sirloin steaks, ¾ inch thick

Directions:
1. Combine the brushing mixture ingredients in a small bowl. Brush the steaks on both sides with the mixture and place on the broiling rack with a pan underneath.
2. BROIL 4 minutes, remove from the oven, turn with tongs, brush the top and sides, and broil again for 4 minutes, or until done to your preference. To use the brushing mixture as a sauce or gravy, pour the mixture into a baking pan.
3. BROIL the mixture for 6 minutes, or until it begins to bubble.

Stuffed Bell Peppers

Servings: 4
Cooking Time: 10 Minutes

Ingredients:
- ¼ pound lean ground pork
- ¾ pound lean ground beef
- ¼ cup onion, minced
- 1 15-ounce can Red Gold crushed tomatoes
- 1 teaspoon Worcestershire sauce
- 1 teaspoon barbeque seasoning
- 1 teaspoon honey
- ½ teaspoon dried basil
- ½ cup cooked brown rice
- ½ teaspoon garlic powder
- ½ teaspoon oregano
- ½ teaspoon salt
- 2 small bell peppers

Directions:
1. Place pork, beef, and onion in air fryer oven baking pan and air-fry at 360°F for 5 minutes.
2. Stir to break apart chunks and cook 3 more minutes. Continue cooking and stirring in 2-minute intervals until meat is well done. Remove from pan and drain.
3. In a small saucepan, combine the tomatoes, Worcestershire, barbeque seasoning, honey, and basil. Stir well to mix in honey and seasonings.
4. In a large bowl, combine the cooked meat mixture, rice, garlic powder, oregano, and salt. Add ¼ cup of the seasoned crushed tomatoes. Stir until well mixed.
5. Cut peppers in half and remove stems and seeds.
6. Stuff each pepper half with one fourth of the meat mixture.
7. Place the peppers in air fryer oven and air-fry for 10 minutes, until peppers are crisp tender.
8. Heat remaining tomato sauce. Serve peppers with warm sauce spooned over top.

Traditional Pot Roast

Servings: 6
Cooking Time: 75 Minutes

Ingredients:

- 2 tablespoons olive oil
- 1 teaspoon garlic powder
- 1 teaspoon fresh thyme, chopped
- ¼ teaspoon sea salt
- ¼ teaspoon freshly ground black pepper
- 1 (3-pound) beef rump roast

Directions:

1. Preheat the toaster oven to 350°F on CONVECTION BAKE for 5 minutes.
2. In a small bowl, stir the oil, garlic, thyme, salt, and pepper. Spread the mixture all over the beef.
3. Place the air-fryer basket in the baking tray and place the beef in the basket.
4. In position 1, bake for 1 hour and 15 minutes until browned and the internal temperature reaches 145°F for medium.
5. Let the roast rest 10 minutes and serve.

RECIPES INDEX

A
Air-fried Potato Salad 8
Almond Crab Cakes 67
Asparagus Fries 16

B
Baked Custard 80
Baked Mac And Cheese 13
Baked Tomato Casserole 52
Beef Vegetable Stew 101
Beer-baked Pork Tenderloin 105
Blackberry Pie 84
Blackened Catfish 61
Blueberry Crumbles 77
Bourbon Bread Pudding 76
Bourbon Broiled Steak 107
Brazilian Cheese Bread (pão De Queijo) 23
Broiled Chipotle Tilapia With Avocado Sauce 54

C
California Burritos 99
Cheese Arancini 28
Cheesy Zucchini Squash Casserole 21
Chewy Coconut Cake 83
Chicken Adobo 36
Chicken Cordon Bleu 38

Chicken Fried Steak 103
Chicken Pot Pie 33
Chicken Potpie 40
Chicken Ranch Roll-ups 45
Chocolate Chip Banana Muffins 88
Chocolate Cupcakes With Salted Caramel Buttercream 78
Cinnamon Pita Chips 27
Cinnamon Toast 89
Coconut Shrimp 69
Coffee Cake 91
Connecticut Garden Chowder 56
Couscous-stuffed Poblano Peppers 47
Crispy "fried" Chicken 35
Crispy Lamb Shoulder Chops 98
Crispy Pecan Fish 68
Crispy Smoked Pork Chops 106

E
Easy Churros 75
Easy Oven Lasagne 51
Easy Peach Turnovers 82
Empty-the-refrigerator Roasted Vegetables 10

F
Fiery Bacon-wrapped Dates 22

Flaky Granola 94

Florentine Stuffed Tomatoes 17

Fried Green Tomatoes 25

Fried Mozzarella Sticks 20

Frozen Brazo De Mercedes 72

G

Golden Seasoned Chicken Wings 39

Granola Three Ways 31

Green Onion Pancakes 85

Grilled Ham & Muenster Cheese On Raisin Bread 24

H

Honey-glazed Ginger Pork Meatballs 55

I

I Forgot To Thaw—garlic Capered Chicken Thighs 41

Italian Baked Chicken 37

K

Kasha Loaf 49

L

Lamb Curry 104

Lemon Blueberry Scones 87

Lemon-dill Salmon Burgers 70

Lemon-roasted Salmon Fillets 71

Lentil "meat" Loaf 9

Light Trout Amandine 62

Lima Bean And Artichoke Casserole 57

N

Not Key Lime, Lime Pie 81

O

Okra Chips 29

Orange-glazed Brownies 73

Oven-crisped Chicken 42

Oysters Broiled In Wine Sauce 63

P

Parmesan Asparagus 12

Pecan-crusted Tilapia 64

Popovers 90

Q

Quick Shrimp Scampi 66

R

Roasted Corn Salad 15

Roasted Eggplant Halves With Herbed Ricotta 14

S

Salmon Salad With Steamboat Dressing 19

Salt And Pepper Baked Potatoes 11

Sausage Cheese Pinwheels 30

Scones 74

Sesame-crusted Tuna Steaks **65**

Slow Cooked Carnitas **100**

Slow Cooker Chicken Philly Cheesesteak Sandwich **46**

Smokehouse-style Beef Ribs **102**

Spanako Pizza **50**

Spicy Fish Street Tacos With Sriracha Slaw **59**

Spicy Sweet Potatoes **18**

Spinach, Tomato & Feta Quiche **92**

Strawberry Pie **95**

Stuffed Bell Peppers **108**

Sun-dried Tomato Pizza **58**

Sweet Potato Fries With Sweet And Spicy Dipping Sauce **26**

Sweet-and-sour Chicken **43**

T

Traditional Pot Roast **109**

Turkey Sausage Cassoulet **34**

W

Walnut Pancake **97**

Y

Yeast Dough For Two Pizzas **53**

Yogurt Bread **86**

Yogurt Cheese Spread **96**

Lightning Source UK Ltd.
Milton Keynes UK
UKHW030655250123
415939UK00009B/471